'International trade remains a cornerstone of economic advancement. As global commerce grows increasingly interconnected, influential, and shaped by business strategies, policies, and complex regulations, an interdisciplinary understanding is more critical than ever. With rigorous theories, current data, and real-world relevance, this book serves as an essential resource for policymakers, practitioners, and academics seeking to understand today's global trade environment'.

Krirkkrai Jirapaet
Former Minister of Commerce, Thailand
Former Permanent Secretary, Ministry of Commerce, Thailand
Former Ambassador of Thailand to the WTO

'International trade is best understood through multiple lenses, yet the legal dimension remains under-integrated in many international business studies. This book brings together international business, economics, trade policies, and legal frameworks in a cohesive and practical way. Clear, insightful, and highly useful for professionals and academics in cross-border trade'.

Sorachon Boonsong
Partner, Baker McKenzie (Bangkok)
Director and Secretary, The Cambridge Thai Foundation

'A rigorous yet accessible foundation for understanding international trade, framed by essential 'why' questions – why it matters for individuals, firms, countries, and the legal frameworks that govern it. The book also highlights how responsibly managed trade can foster inclusive and sustainable development. A recommended read for those seeking to understand the holistic picture of international trade'.

Nitinant Wisaweisuan
Former Dean, Puey Ungphakorn School of Development Studies,
Thammasat University, Thailand
Lecturer in Economics

'A well-structured and reader-friendly analysis of international trade. A practical and comprehensive guide to navigating today's complex global markets'.

Chantapat Panjamanond
Minister (Commercial), Office of Commercial Affairs,
Royal Thai Embassy, Tokyo
Author of *Global Trends for Thai Products: A Guide to Survival and Growth for Entrepreneurs*

AF737031

INTERNATIONAL TRADE ESSENTIALS

This book will help us understand how international trade shapes our lives, our economies, and our future. By weaving together insights from business, economics, and law, this work offers a clear, practical, and relevant perspective on international trade.

It covers topics including global trade ecosystem, internationalisation, international trade theories, policies and measures, Incoterms, customs formalities process, key contracts, and international trade and sustainability.

With a focus on translating theoretical principles into real-world applications, this book equips students and practitioners with essential knowledge and practical tools to navigate the complexities of international trade and global business.

Nuntana Udomkit is Associate Professor of Business Administration at Mahidol University International College, Mahidol University, Thailand. She earned her Ph.D. in Economics and International Development from the University of Bath, United Kingdom, along with a law degree and specialised certificates in International Trade and International Trade Law.

Before joining academia, she gained professional experience at the Bank of Thailand, the Ministry of Commerce, and in legal practice. She now teaches courses in Global Trade, Policies and Regulations, and Internationalisation Strategy.

INTERNATIONAL TRADE ESSENTIALS

An Integrated Approach Across Business, Economics, and Law

Nuntana Udomkit

Mahidol University International College,
Mahidol University, Thailand

Routledge
Taylor & Francis Group
LONDON AND NEW YORK

Designed cover image: DINphotogallery

First published 2026
by Routledge
4 Park Square, Milton Park, Abingdon, Oxon OX14 4RN

and by Routledge
605 Third Avenue, New York, NY 10158

Routledge is an imprint of the Taylor & Francis Group, an informa business

© 2026 Nuntana Udomkit

The right of Nuntana Udomkit to be identified as author of this work has been asserted in accordance with sections 77 and 78 of the Copyright, Designs and Patents Act 1988.

All rights reserved. No part of this book may be reprinted or reproduced or utilised in any form or by any electronic, mechanical, or other means, now known or hereafter invented, including photocopying and recording, or in any information storage or retrieval system, without permission in writing from the publishers.

Trademark notice: Product or corporate names may be trademarks or registered trademarks, and are used only for identification and explanation without intent to infringe.

British Library Cataloguing-in-Publication Data
A catalogue record for this book is available from the British Library

ISBN: 978-1-032-88017-4 (hbk)
ISBN: 978-1-032-88016-7 (pbk)
ISBN: 978-1-003-53587-4 (ebk)

DOI: 10.4324/9781003535874

Typeset in Galliard
by Apex CoVantage, LLC

To my beloved father,

who instilled in me a lifelong curiosity to explore,
the discipline to read, and the courage to write.
Though you are no longer here, your words and spirit
continue to guide every page of this work.
I hope, somewhere out there, you can read this book
and know that so much of it began with you.

CONTENTS

FIGURES

TABLES

ACKNOWLEDGEMENTS

This book is the culmination of years of learning, working, reflecting, and growing. I am indebted to the many individuals and communities who have shaped my journey and made this work possible.

First and foremost, I would like to thank my family, teachers, professors, and advisors, from both formal and informal learning spaces, who helped lay the foundation of my knowledge. Your generosity in sharing your wisdom has left a lasting imprint on my being, shaping how I think, live, and work.

I am deeply grateful to the Royal Thai Government and the Japan International Cooperation Agency (JICA) for their generous scholarships that enabled my access to quality education, which has profoundly shaped my outlook and aspirations. These opportunities have reinforced my conviction that education transforms lives. It empowers, enlightens, and endows individuals with the wisdom to grow and contribute meaningfully to society.

To all the inspiring leaders, mentors, supervisors, and colleagues I have had the privilege to work with, thank you for your trust, encouragement, and the chance to be involved in so many meaningful and challenging projects. The insights and experiences gained from these moments have directly influenced the ideas and perspectives presented in this book. I am especially grateful for the opportunity to work in the field of international trade at the Ministry of Commerce and to serve as a lawyer managing several challenging international trade disputes. These roles deepened my understanding of the complex interconnections between global business, public policies, and legal frameworks. Today, as a researcher, educator, and lifelong learner, I continue to expand and refine my insights.

Finally, I extend my heartfelt thanks to all my research assistants, peer reviewers, the publisher, and esteemed professional colleagues whose critical observations, thought-provoking insights, and invaluable feedback have greatly enriched the scholarly quality of this work. I also wish to acknowledge the role of artificial intelligence tools, which have provided practical support in preliminary research and linguistic refinement of this book.

GLOSSARY

AANZFTA	ASEAN-Australia-New Zealand Free Trade Agreement
ACFTA	ASEAN-China Free Trade Agreement
ADB	Asian Development Bank
AEC	ASEAN Economic Community
AfCFTA	African Continental Free Trade Agreement
AFTA	ASEAN Free Trade Agreement
AIFTA	ASEAN-India Free Trade Agreement
AJCEP	ASEAN-Japan Comprehensive Economic Partnership
AKFTA	ASEAN-Korea Free Trade Agreement
AmCham	American Chamber of Commerce
APEC	Asia-Pacific Economic Cooperation
ASEAN	Association of Southeast Asian Nations
AWB	Air Waybill
B/L	Bill of Lading
BOT	Balance of Trade
CAN	Comunidad Andina/Andean Community
CARICOM	Caribbean Community
CBAM	Carbon Border Adjustment Mechanism
CFR	Cost and Freight
CICC	China International Commercial Court
CIF	Cost, Insurance, and Freight
CIP	Carriage and Insurance Paid To
CISG	United Nations Convention on Contracts for the International Sale of Goods
CITES	Convention on International Trade in Endangered Species
CNIL	Commission Nationale de l'Informatique et des Libertés

C/O	Certificate of Origin
CPT	Carriage Paid To
CPTPP	Comprehensive and Progressive Agreement for Trans-Pacific Partnership
CSR	Corporate Social Responsibility
D/C	Documentary Collection
DAP	Delivered at Place
DDP	Delivered Duty Paid
DPU	Delivered at Place Unloaded
EAC	East African Community
ECOWAS	Economic Community of West African States
EFTA	European Free Trade Association
ESG	Environmental, Social, and Governance
EU	European Union
EUDR	European Union Deforestation Regulation
EV	Eclectic Vehicle
EVFTA	European Union-Vietnam Free Trade Agreement
EXW	Ex Works
FAS	Free Alongside Ship
FCA	Free Carrier
FDI	Foreign Direct Investment
FOB	Free on Board
FSC	Forest Stewardship Council
FTA	Free Trade Agreement
GATT	General Agreement on Tariffs and Trade
GDP	Gross Domestic Product
GDPR	General Data Protection Regulation
GVC	Global Value Chain
HS Code	Harmonized System Code
ICC (A)	Institute Cargo Clauses A
ICC (B)	Institute Cargo Clauses B
ICC (C)	Institute Cargo Clauses C
ICC	International Chamber of Commerce
ILO	International Labour Organization
IMF	International Monetary Fund
Incoterms	International Commercial Terms
ISO	International Organization for Standardization
ITA	International Trade Administration (US Department of Commerce)
ITC	International Trade Centre
IUU	Illegal, Unreported, and Unregulated (Fishing)
JETRO	Japan External Trade Organization

JTEPA	Japan-Thailand Economic Partnership Agreement
JV	Joint Venture
L/C	Letter of Credit
LCIA	London Court of International Arbitration
LCIA	London Court of International Arbitration
METI	Ministry of Economy, Trade and Industry (Japan)
MNC	Multinational Corporation
MNE	Multinational Enterprise
MOFCOM	Ministry of Commerce (China)
MSC	Marine Stewardship Council
MTI	Ministry of Trade and Industry (Singapore)
NAFTA	North American Free Trade Agreement
NGO	Non-Governmental Organization
OECD	Organization for Economic Co-operation and Development
PESTEL	Political, Economic, Social, Technological, Environmental, and Legal analysis
RCEP	Regional Comprehensive Economic Partnership
R&D	Research and Development
SIAC	Singapore International Arbitration Centre
SMC	Singapore Mediation Centre
SME	Small and Medium-sized Enterprise
TPP	Trans-Pacific Partnership
UCP 600	Uniform Customs and Practice for Documentary Credits (ICC Publication No. 600)
UN	United Nations
UNCTAD	United Nations Conference on Trade and Development
USMCA	United States-Mexico-Canada Agreement
USTR	Office of the United States Trade Representative
VER	Voluntary Export Restraint
WCO	World Customs Organization
WEEE	Waste Electrical and Electronic Equipment Directive
WTO	World Trade Organization

PART 1

Why Does International Trade Matter for Us All?

1

INTRODUCTION

Can We Imagine a Future Without International Trade?

Learning Objectives

1 Understand the significance of international trade in shaping and connecting global economies.
2 Critically evaluate the impacts of globalisation on international trade.

In today's globalised economy, international trade has become so deeply embedded in everyday life that it shapes the products and services we rely on from dawn to dusk. For instance, in my own daily routine, I begin the morning by waking up to the alarm on my Samsung mobile phone, a South Korean brand whose phones are mainly manufactured in Vietnam. As I prepare for the day, I brush my teeth with Sensodyne toothpaste, a brand originating in the United Kingdom and distributed worldwide. My morning coffee is brewed using beans from Mondulkiri, a region in north-eastern Cambodia known for its rich and earthy flavour.

For transportation, I drive a Subaru, a vehicle from the Japanese automaker Subaru, built at its plant in Malaysia. At lunchtime, I often have lunch at the college's canteen, where many of the fruits and vegetables are imported from China. During the workday, I rely on a Microsoft Surface device, developed in the United States and manufactured through complex international supply chains. In the evening, I like to unwind with a good meal, occasionally pairing Chilean wine with Argentine beef. To end the day, I rest on an IKEA bed, a symbol of Swedish home innovation and efficient global production networks.

Historically speaking, trade has long served as a conduit for the transmission of ideas, technologies, and even food culture across the world. Papermaking, which originated during the Han dynasty in China, reached the Islamic world

DOI: 10.4324/9781003535874-2

by the eighth century and spread to Europe via Al-Andalus[1] (Bloom, 2001). Chinese porcelain, refined during the Tang and Song dynasties, travelled westward through overland and maritime trade (Finlay, 2010). Chili peppers, native to the Americas, were introduced to Asia by Portuguese traders in the sixteenth century and quickly became integral to cuisines in India, China, and Korea (Andrews, 1999).

From an economic standpoint, international trade serves as a powerful engine for economic growth. By participating in trade, countries can extend their markets beyond domestic boundaries. This increased economic activity contributes to job creation, higher income levels, and improved living standards. Singapore provides a compelling example of these dynamics in action. Despite having limited natural resources and a small domestic market, Singapore strategically embraced free trade as a cornerstone of its economic policy. Through early adoption of trade liberalisation, openness, and global connectivity, the country successfully positioned itself as a major hub for international commerce and investment (Lee, 2000). Its proactive approach attracted foreign capital, fostered industrial development, and propelled it to become one of the world's most competitive economies. Today, Singapore's extensive network of free trade agreements (FTAs) continues to play a pivotal role in sustaining its economic prosperity (World Bank Group, n.d.-b).

From a business perspective, international trade offers companies access to broader customer bases, enabling them to tap into new markets and diversify their revenue streams. Multinational corporations (MNCs) underscore the strategic importance of international market engagement, with global operations not only supporting their business structures but also serving as key drivers of sustained growth and competitiveness. For instance, McDonald's generated approximately 60% of its $23.18 billion revenue from international markets in 2022 (McDonald's, 2023). Similarly, Coca-Cola derived the majority of its $43.00 billion revenue from regions outside North America (Coca-Cola Company, 2023). Toyota reported that nearly half of its $279.3 billion in fiscal year 2022 sales originated from international markets (Toyota Motor Corporation, 2023). Samsung Electronics generated around 84% of its $234.1 billion revenue from international sales in 2022 (Samsung Electronics, 2023). Nike obtained 57% of its $51.2 billion revenue in 2023 from foreign markets (Nike, 2023). BMW Group attributed the majority of its $152.2 billion revenue in 2022 to exports (BMW Group, 2023). Likewise, Moët Hennessy Louis Vuitton SE (LVMH) reported that over 90% of its $84.5 billion revenue in 2022 was generated from international markets (LVMH, 2023).

It is worth noting that large corporations rely heavily on global value chains (GVCs), underscoring the interdependence of multiple players across borders. For example, Apple sources components from over 40 countries and assembles devices across global manufacturing facilities, primarily in China, India, Vietnam, and Brazil (Miller & Venugopalan, 2025), while Toyota operates a complex international supply network, manufacturing vehicles across different continents to optimise local efficiencies and market access (Edward, 2024). Similarly, fashion giant Zara exemplifies the modern trade model through its fast-fashion strategy, leveraging international sourcing and agile logistics to rapidly deliver products to markets worldwide (Pons & Reid, 2024).

However, while MNCs dominate GVCs and often command the spotlight in discussions of international trade, they are not the only drivers of cross-border commerce. These global networks also depend heavily on the contributions of small and medium-sized enterprises (SMEs), which form critical links within supply chains and provide essential inputs, services, and labour. SMEs play a vital role in shaping international trade dynamics, particularly in developing economies, where they contribute significantly to employment and economic output. In Cambodia, for example, garment and apparel SMEs are integral to global apparel supply chains. As of December 2023, this sector contributed roughly 10% to Cambodia's gross domestic product (GDP) and accounted for 62.26% of the country's total exports, employing 918,718 workers across 1,680 garment and bag factories (Council for the Development of Cambodia, n.d.).

Global Trade Contemporary Landscape: Size, Products, and Players

International trade has experienced remarkable growth and transformation over the past centuries. Components and finished goods now criss-cross multiple borders before reaching consumers. Advances in transportation, communication, and information technologies have enabled the development of complex global supply chains. Moreover, the twenty-first century has witnessed rapid growth of the digital economy, profoundly transforming the nature of international trade. Online marketplaces and digital platforms have enabled cross-border e-commerce and digital services trade, connected businesses, and expanded market access for SMEs to consumers across the world.

Global trade has substantially increased in its significance as a share of global GDP, rising from less than 10% in the 1950s to nearly 60% in 2024 (World Bank Group, n.d.-e). According to World Trade Organization (WTO) (2025), global merchandise exports totalled approximately $24.5 trillion in 2024. The ten largest exporting countries significantly dominated this landscape, accounting for roughly 50% of global exports. China led this group with exports valued at $3.6 trillion, representing 14.6% of the global share, followed by the United States at $2.1 trillion (8.4%) and Germany at $1.7 trillion (6.9%). Other notable exporting economies included the Netherlands, Japan, South Korea, Italy, Belgium, France, and Hong Kong SAR.

On the import side, global trade in 2024 reached approximately $24.8 trillion. The ten largest importing countries also represented about 50% of the global imports. The United States topped the list, importing goods valued at \$3.4 trillion (13.6%), driven primarily by strong consumer demand. China followed at \$2.6 trillion (10.4%), with Germany importing goods valued at \$1.4 trillion (5.7%). Other leading importers included the United Kingdom, the Netherlands, France, Japan, India, Hong Kong SAR, and Mexico.

Manufactured goods, including electrical machinery and equipment, machinery, vehicles, represent approximately 63% of global merchandise exports, followed by fuels and mining products (approximately 21%), agricultural products (approximately 10%), and other goods (approximately 6%) (World Trade Organization (WTO), 2023b).

Agricultural products remain economically and socially significant, serving as key sources of export revenue for the producing countries and essential elements of food security for the importing nations. Everyday items like corn, wheat, rice, meat, sugar, cotton, and spices are some of the most traded agricultural products globally. Maize, wheat, and rice serve as foundational dietary staples for billions. The United States, Brazil, and Argentina dominate maize exports, while Mexico, Japan, and South Korea are major importers.[2] Wheat is primarily exported by countries such as Russia, Canada, and Australia, and imported heavily by Egypt, Indonesia, and Türkiye.[3] Rice, with India and Thailand as its leading exporters, is a lifeline for countries like China, Nigeria, and the Philippines.[4]

Soybeans and oilseeds are critical for food-processing industries, animal feed, and biofuel production. The United States and Brazil are top soybean exporters, supplying China, the world's largest importer.[5] Brazil, the United States, and the European Union (EU) are major poultry exporters, with China and Japan among the key importers.[6] Brazil dominates sugar exports, while countries like Indonesia and the United States are key buyers.[7] Spices, primarily exported by India and Vietnam, cater to demand in the European Union and North America.[8] Cotton supports the global textile industry, with the United States, India, and Uzbekistan among the top exporters, and China and Bangladesh as key importers feeding into their textile manufacturing hubs.[9]

About This Book

Given the profound impact of international trade, its study naturally spans multiple academic fields, where each discipline contributes unique insights and focal points. In business studies, international trade is integrated into the broader context of international business management and international entrepreneurship. Key topics include market entry strategies, internationalisation strategy, global supply chain management, cross-border mergers and acquisitions, and the role of multinational enterprises (MNEs). Case studies are commonly employed to demonstrate how firms engage with foreign markets, mitigate risks, and adapt to cultural differences in the pursuit of international growth.

In economics, international trade is typically viewed through both theoretical and policy-oriented lenses. Core areas include international trade theories, trade policy instruments, international trade agreements, regional economic integration, and their effects on economic growth, employment, and income distribution.

In legal studies, international trade focuses on the contractual and regulatory frameworks that facilitate cross-border transactions. Key areas include Incoterms, international sales contracts, transportation and carriage of goods, cargo insurance, customs regulations, and dispute resolution mechanisms.

The overarching aim of this book is to seamlessly integrate business, economics, and legal aspects of international trade, striking a balance between academic rigor and an engaging, reader-friendly narrative. It seeks to provide both theoretical underpinnings and practical applications, with the ultimate goal of offering a strong foundational understanding of global commerce for international entrepreneurs, policymakers, practitioners, as well as advanced-level students.

This book serves readers valuable insights through questions that everyone can relate to. Part 1 begins by addressing the question *Why does international trade matter to us all?*, illustrating both the significance and the vast scale of global commerce.

Part 2 explores *why international trade matters for firms*, examining trade through the lens of international business management. It begins with the chapter titled 'Unveiling the Global Trade Ecosystem', outlining its key players and their roles in shaping the dynamics of global trade. At the international level, institutions like the World Trade Organization (WTO), World Customs Organization (WCO), European Union, and ASEAN play important roles in their regulatory and collaborative functions. Nationally, governments and their regulatory bodies play crucial roles in facilitating and regulating trade. Meanwhile, the private sector, including carriers, banks, freight forwarders, exporters, importers, distributors, and logistics companies, forms the operational backbone. Understanding the synergies and interdependencies within these tiers is essential for comprehending the intricate dynamics that underpin the global trade landscape.

The chapter titled 'Essentials of Internationalisation Strategy' delves into various international entry modes as well as the key barriers and risks businesses encountered during the internationalisation journey. It is followed by 'Internationalisation: Key Issues and Challenges', which highlights the major challenges associated with global expansion and presents strategies for managing risks in international trade.

Part 3 addresses the question *Why does international trade matter for countries?* This section deepens the understanding of international trade from an economic perspective. It starts with the chapter titled 'The Economic Significance of International Trade', which emphasises its pivotal role as a catalyst for economic growth. This is followed by 'International Trade's Ideologies and Theoretical Compass', which reviews historical trade theories, from mercantilism to free trade, providing a contextual foundation for understanding modern trade ideologies, policies, and their dynamics. Finally, 'International Trade Policies and Measures' explores key international trade measures employed by governments.

Part 4 asks *Why do international trade laws and regulations matter?* It begins with 'Key Principles of International Commercial Terms (Incoterms®)', explaining their application in defining the responsibilities and risks of exporters and importers, as well as their impact on pricing, logistics, and risk management. Following this, the focus shifts to 'Customs Formalities Process', including an overview of customs procedures, the structure and global significance of the Harmonized System (HS) for product classification, and the key documents typically required to facilitate the customs clearance process. The section concludes with 'Key Contracts in International Trade', examining of essential contracts in international trade and mechanisms for resolving international trade disputes.

Part 5, *Why Does Sustainable Trade Matter?*, shifts the focus towards the transformative potential of international trade as a catalyst for positive economic, social, and environmental impacts. 'International Trade for a Sustainable World' highlights that trade is not merely an economic transaction but also a powerful force capable of shaping a more equitable, inclusive, and sustainable global economic landscape.

Notes

1 Al-Andalus was the name given to the regions of the Iberian Peninsula that came under Islamic rule between 711 and 1492 CE, encompassing large parts of what are now Spain and Portugal. During its peak, Al-Andalus became one of the most vibrant centres of intellectual, scientific, and cultural activity in medieval Europe. Al-Andalus served as a crucial link between the Islamic world and Christian Europe. Important scientific and technological innovations, such as advances in mathematics, medicine, astronomy, and papermaking, reached Europe through this cultural exchange (Fletcher, 2006).

2 For a detailed overview of global corn trade, see Observatory of Economic Complexity (OEC). (n.d.-a). https://oec.world/en/profile/hs/corn

3 For a detailed overview of global wheat trade, see OEC. (n.d.-j). https://oec.world/en/profile/hs/wheat

4 For a detailed overview of global rice trade, see OEC. (n.d.-e). https://oec.world/en/profile/hs/rice

5 For a detailed overview of global soybeans trade, see OEC. (n.d.-g). https://oec.world/en/profile/hs/soybeans

6 For a detailed overview of global poultry meat trade, see OEC. (n.d.-c). https://oec.world/en/profile/hs/poultry-meat
7 For a detailed overview of global sugar trade, see OEC. (n.d.-d). https://oec.world/en/profile/hs/raw-sugar
8 For a detailed overview of global spices trade, see OEC. (n.d.-h). https://oec.world/en/profile/hs/spices
9 For a detailed overview of global cotton trade, see OEC. (n.d.-b). https://oec.world/en/profile/hs/cotton

PART 2

Why Does International Trade Matter for Firms?

2

UNVEILING THE GLOBAL TRADE ECOSYSTEM

Learning Objectives

1 Understand the international trade ecosystem, including international institutions, governments, and private sector as well as their pivotal roles in regulating, fostering, and shaping the global trade ecosystem.
2 Recognise the multifaceted interactions among stakeholders in the international trade ecosystem and appreciate how these interactions collectively shape the functioning of international commerce.

The Complex Web Behind a Single International Transaction

Imagine a Japanese food importer importing frozen shrimp from a Thai food processing company. To make this seemingly simple transaction possible, a network of interconnected players must coordinate closely.

1 The Thai exporter and the Japanese importer negotiate the terms of sale, including product specifications, pricing, shipment conditions, and compliance with Japanese food safety standards.
2 The bank provides trade finance instruments to facilitate the business.
3 A freight forwarder organises the transportation of the frozen shrimp, ensuring the goods are handled under controlled temperature conditions, and arranges shipment with a carrier.

DOI: 10.4324/9781003535874-4

4 Before leaving Thailand, the shipment must pass through the Thai customs formalities process.
5 Upon arrival in Japan, the shipment undergoes inspection by Japanese customs, which enforces strict food safety laws.
6 Duty and taxes are assessed based on the declared value and tariff rates applicable to frozen seafood products.
7 Logistics companies handle the inland transport and cold storage distribution to supermarkets, restaurants, and other buyers in Japan.
8 Throughout the process, government authorities in both Thailand and Japan ensure compliance with national regulations and obligations under international agreements, such as those of the WTO and the Japan–Thailand Economic Partnership Agreement (JTEPA).

If any part of this complex chain fails, the entire transaction can collapse, leading to costly delays, financial losses, and strained commercial relationships. It is therefore vital that every actor and institution functions smoothly to sustain global commerce.

The international trade ecosystem is a highly interconnected and dynamic network that brings together a wide range of key players who collectively enable the exchange of goods and services across borders. It encompasses multiple layers of interaction – from international organisations that establish common rules, agreements, and platforms for cooperation among member countries, to national governments that design and implement trade policies reflecting their economic and strategic priorities. At the operational level, businesses drive the actual movement of goods and services, responding to consumer demands. Each participant plays a distinct yet interdependent role, highlighting the complexity of international commerce and its reliance on coordinated efforts among diverse actors.

International Level

Various international organisations play a pivotal role in shaping the rules and dynamics of global trade. Notable examples include:

World Trade Organization (WTO): The WTO was established on January 1, 1995, succeeding the General Agreement on Tariffs and Trade (GATT), which had been created in 1947 (World Trade Organization, n.d.-a). The WTO is headquartered in Geneva, Switzerland, and currently has 164 member countries, representing over 98% of global trade (World Trade Organization, n.d.-a, n.d.-b).

The WTO is a global institution that deals with the rules of trade between nations. Its main role is to ensure that international trade flows as smoothly, predictably, and freely as possible. It administers a series of trade agreements that cover goods, services, intellectual property rights, and other areas critical to global trade. Its function also includes operating a binding dispute settlement mechanism. When member countries disagree on the interpretation or application of WTO agreements, they can bring disputes before the WTO's Dispute Settlement Body, which adjudicates the cases and ensures compliance with rulings. The WTO also serves as a vital forum for member countries to negotiate the reduction or elimination of trade barriers and to update trade rules as necessary, providing a common institutional framework for conducting trade relations among members (World Trade Organization, n.d.-a, n.d.-b).

United Nations Conference on Trade and Development (UNCTAD): UNCTAD is a permanent intergovernmental body within the United Nations. It was established by the UN General Assembly in 1964. It currently comprises 195 member states and operates a permanent secretariat headquartered in Geneva, Switzerland. UNCTAD's mandate spans the interconnected areas of trade, investment, finance, technology, and sustainable development. Its core mission is to promote development through trade by helping developing countries maximise the benefits of globalisation. It conducts extensive research and analysis, publishing data and studies on global economic trends, trade policies, and development strategies and proposes policy tools aimed at fostering inclusive and sustainable economic growth in the Global South (UNCTAD, n.d.).

World Customs Organization (WCO): The WCO is an independent intergovernmental body centrally focused on enhancing the effectiveness and efficiency of customs administrations worldwide. It was established in 1952 as the Customs Co-operation Council (CCC) and later renamed the World Customs Organization in 1994. The WCO is headquartered in Brussels, Belgium, and currently has 185 members, representing over 98% of international trade (WCO, n.d.-a).

The WCO plays a leading role in developing international standards for customs procedures. One of its key contributions is the creation and maintenance of the Harmonized Commodity Description and Coding System, commonly known as the HS,[1] which standardises the classification of traded goods. These standards simplify and harmonise customs processes, thereby facilitating international trade by reducing costs and administrative burdens across countries. Beyond facilitating trade, the WCO focuses on securing the international trade supply chain. It develops policies and standards aimed at combating illegal activities such as smuggling, customs fraud, and other cross-border crimes. The WCO also supports customs administrations in enforcing regulations related to the import, export, and transit of dangerous goods, hazardous materials, and substances harmful to health and the environment, promoting secure, efficient, and lawful international trade (WCO, 2023, n.d.-a).

International Trade Centre (ITC): The ITC is a joint agency of the WTO and the United Nations (through UNCTAD), originally established as the International Trade Information Centre in 1964 and formally reconstituted as the ITC in 1968, headquartered in Geneva, Switzerland. ITC's mission is to foster inclusive and sustainable economic development by helping micro, small, and medium-sized enterprises in developing and transition economies connect with global markets. Its core functions include delivering market and trade intelligence, building export readiness capacity, and providing technical assistance to enhance trade facilitation and competitiveness (International Trade Centre, n.d.).

International Chamber of Commerce (ICC): The ICC, founded in 1919 and headquartered in Paris, France, is the world's largest business organisation, representing over 45 million companies across more than 170 countries. The ICC develops globally recognised commercial rules and standards, such as Incoterms®[2] and Uniform Customs and Practice for Documentary Credits (UCP 600),[3] to simplify international trade transactions. It also operates the ICC International Court of Arbitration, a leading institution for resolving commercial disputes (ICC, n.d.-a).

Beyond institutions that directly govern trade, several international organisations play an indirect yet essential role in strengthening global commerce. For instance, the *World Bank* provides both financial and technical assistance to enhance trade infrastructure, improve logistics, and support development in developing economies (World Bank Group, n.d.-c). Similarly, the *International Monetary Fund (IMF)* contributes to global trade by maintaining monetary stability and providing financial assistance to countries facing balance-of-payments difficulties. By stabilising national economies, the IMF indirectly fosters predictable and smoother trade flows (IMF, n.d.). At the regional level, the *Asian Development Bank (ADB)* supports trade facilitation programmes, infrastructure development, and regional integration projects across Asia and the Pacific. These initiatives enhance the competitiveness and capacity of member economies, enabling them to participate more actively in GVCs (Asian Development Bank, n.d.).

National Level

While international organisations set the fundamental frameworks that govern global trade, the practical implementation of these rules occurs predominantly at the national level. National governments, through their ministries and regulatory agencies, play a critical role in facilitating, regulating, and promoting international trade.

Governments and their various ministries and regulatory bodies – typically those responsible for trade, commerce, foreign affairs, agriculture, industry, transport, and logistics – coordinate efforts to negotiate trade agreements, manage customs operations, and ensure legal compliance with national regulations related to security, food safety, product standards, and necessary licensing and permits.

For instance, in the United States, the Department of Commerce, particularly through its International Trade Administration (ITA), handles trade and investment promotion activities, while the Office of the United States Trade Representative (USTR) is responsible for developing and recommending trade policy to the President, conducting trade negotiations, and coordinating trade policy across the federal government (US Department of Commerce, n.d.; Office of the US Trade Representative, n.d.a).

In China, the Ministry of Commerce (MOFCOM) administers international trade policies, promotes foreign trade, and regulates market competition (Ministry of Commerce of the People's Republic of China, n.d.). In Japan, the Ministry of Economy, Trade and Industry (METI) leads efforts in shaping economic and industrial policy, implementing trade agreements, overseeing import and export regulations, and enhancing the global competitiveness of Japanese industries (Ministry of Economy, Trade and Industry, Japan, n.d.). METI plays a critical role in negotiating economic partnership agreements, promoting trade liberalisation, and coordinating foreign investment policies. In Singapore, trade and economic development fall under the purview of the Ministry of Trade and Industry (MTI). The MTI formulates policies to strengthen Singapore's position as a global trading hub and oversees agencies such as Enterprise Singapore and Singapore Customs, which are tasked with supporting trade promotion, innovation, and ensuring compliance with customs regulations (Ministry of Trade and Industry, Singapore (MTI), n.d.-a).

It is important to note that the dynamics of international trade are heavily influenced by national economic policies, regulatory frameworks, and broader economic and social conditions. These national-level decisions can trigger significant shifts in global trade patterns and supply chains. For example, China's strategic use of subsidies in sectors such as batteries and electric vehicles (EVs) demonstrates how government intervention can foster rapid industrial growth and create global competitive advantage. Chinese government subsidies have enabled companies to innovate, scale production, and reduce manufacturing costs, making Chinese-made EVs and related components highly competitive in international markets. In response, major economies such as the United States, the European Union, and Canada have imposed or proposed tariffs on imported Chinese batteries and EVs, aiming to counterbalance the perceived market distortions caused by these subsidies (Daly, 2024; The Guardian, 2024; Reuters, 2025a).

In addition to ministries and regulatory agencies, many countries have established specialised dispute resolution bodies or courts to resolve international trade and commercial disputes. These institutions play a critical role in ensuring that trade disputes are resolved fairly, efficiently, and in accordance with national and international law.

Specialised courts provide a judicial framework specifically designed for handling complex cases related to international contracts, shipping, investment, intellectual property, and cross-border commercial disputes. For example, Singapore has the Singapore International Commercial Court (SICC) (Singapore International Commercial Court, n.d.), the United Kingdom has the London Commercial Court (United Kingdom) (UK Judiciary, n.d.), and China has the China International Commercial Court (CICC) (China International Commercial Court, n.d.).

Besides specialised courts, many businesses and legal practitioners increasingly rely on alternative dispute resolution mechanisms, particularly arbitration, as an effective means of resolving international commercial disputes. Prominent arbitral bodies include the International Chamber of Commerce (ICC) in Paris, the London Court of International Arbitration (LCIA), and the Singapore International Arbitration Centre (SIAC). These institutions provide standardised procedural frameworks, qualified arbitrators, and institutional rules that allow parties from diverse legal systems to resolve disputes with enhanced flexibility, neutrality, enforceability, and confidentiality.[4]

Trade Facilitation and Promotion Agencies

Trade facilitation and promotion agencies also play a vital role in supporting international trade. These institutions help businesses navigate regulatory environments, identify market opportunities, and build international partnerships. One major category of such agencies includes Chambers of Commerce and Trade or Industry Associations. These organisations provide support, advocacy, and networking opportunities for businesses engaged in international trade. They act as bridges between the private sector and government, offering members access to trade information, policy updates, export readiness training, and platforms for influencing trade policy. For example, the American Chamber of Commerce (AmCham) – the largest business federation in the United States – represents businesses of all sizes and advocates for pro-trade policies and improved market access for American companies. The AmCham network comprises over 115 chambers in more than 100 countries, supporting US business interests abroad through policy advocacy and networking (AmCham, n.d.). Examples include AmCham Thailand, AmCham Singapore, and AmCham EU. Similarly, German Chambers of Commerce Abroad (AHK or Auslandshandelskammern) operate a global network of chambers with over 140 offices in 92 countries, supporting German businesses in international markets. These chambers provide services such as market entry consulting, legal and regulatory guidance, and matchmaking with local partners, thereby playing a vital role in facilitating bilateral trade and investment (German Chambers of Commerce, n.d.).

In Japan, the Japan External Trade Organization (JETRO), a government-affiliated agency, is dedicated to facilitating mutual trade and investment between Japan and the global economy. JETRO supports Japanese businesses, particularly SMEs, in expanding overseas through trade fairs, business matching, and regulatory guidance. It also plays a pivotal role in attracting foreign direct investment (FDI) into Japan by offering advisory services, market intelligence, and logistical support to foreign companies (JETRO, n.d.). Similarly, in Singapore, the Singapore Business Federation (SBF) actively supports internationalisation through trade missions, advisory services, and engagement with government trade initiatives (Singapore Business Federation, n.d.).

Private Sector

The private sector is the driving engine of international trade. Globally, private enterprises account for more than 80% of cross-border trade flows (World Economic Forum, 2020). They produce, distribute, and market goods and services that move through complex GVCs. Prominent actors include:

Exporters and importers: These businesses form the foundation of international trade by selling goods and services abroad (exporters) or purchasing goods and services from other countries (importers).

Freight forwarders: Freight forwarders serve as intermediaries between shippers and transportation providers, coordinating logistics, preparing transport documentation, managing customs procedures, and ensuring regulatory compliance. Prominent global freight forwarders include DHL Global Forwarding, Kuehne + Nagel, and DB Schenker (Statista, 2023).

Carriers: Several international carriers play a crucial role in facilitating the movement of goods across borders through sea, air, and land transport. In maritime logistics, leading container shipping companies include Maersk Line, Mediterranean Shipping Company (MSC), CMA CGM, and Hapag-Lloyd, which together control a majority share of global container capacity (Alphaliner, 2025; Statista, 2023). In the air freight sector, major carriers include FedEx Express, UPS Airlines, DHL Aviation, and Qatar Airways Cargo (Air Cargo News, 2024). For road and multimodal freight services, companies like DB Schenker, Kuehne + Nagel, XPO Logistics, and DHL Supply Chain integrate warehousing, trucking, and customs brokerage to ensure seamless global supply chain management. These carriers form the backbone of international logistics networks, enabling efficient cross-border commerce.

Warehouse operators: Warehouse operators manage the storage of goods either prior to shipment or after arrival at their destination. They offer warehousing, inventory management, and distribution services.

Customs brokers: Customs brokers specialise in ensuring that goods meet all legal requirements for importation and exportation. They assist businesses in preparing documentation, calculating duties and taxes, and expediting customs clearance processes.

Logistics companies: Logistics providers manage the end-to-end coordination of goods along the supply chain, integrating transport, warehousing, customs clearance, inventory management, and delivery. Leading global logistics companies include DHL Supply Chain, Kuehne + Nagel, and DB Schenker.

Banks and financial institutions: Financial institutions play a critical role in supporting international trade by providing financial assistance and loans, facilitating transactions through instruments such as letters of credit (L/C), trade finance, foreign exchange services, and export credit guarantees.

Insurance companies: Insurance providers mitigate risks associated with international trade by offering coverage for cargo loss, theft, damage, and trade credit risks.

Conclusion

This chapter has provided a foundational understanding of how the international trade ecosystem operates and why it matters. The international trade ecosystem is composed of interlocking roles, relationships, and responsibilities. At its core, it represents the interconnected operations of institutions, governments, and businesses, each shaping and responding to the forces of global commerce. International organisations like the WTO and WCO establish foundational principles, rules, and regulations that enable predictability and cooperation. National governments implement these rules through domestic legislation and trade policy, balancing sovereignty and national interests with international obligations.

Meanwhile, businesses, from small producers to MNCs, serve as the operational engine of trade, delivering products and services that cross borders. Behind the scenes, several actors such as freight forwarders, customs brokers, logistics firms, banks, insurance companies, inspection agencies, and trade chambers play a critical role in ensuring that goods are properly transported, inspected, financed, and documented throughout the international trade process. Each stakeholder in this system plays a distinct but interconnected role, and disruption in any part can ripple through the entire chain, causing delays, inefficiencies, or systemic breakdowns. As global crises – such as pandemics, geopolitical conflicts, and climate change – increasingly expose the fragility of this ecosystem, the need for cooperation, adaptability, and mutual accountability becomes even more apparent.

The next chapter will progress from ecosystem-wide dynamics to firm-level decisions, connecting macro-level trade structures with micro-level business strategy. It explores why and how companies engage with international markets. Specifically, we will examine internationalisation strategies and their significance, assess various market entry modes and their respective advantages and disadvantages, and identify the key barriers and risks businesses face when expanding across borders.

Key Takeaway

1. International trade operates within a complex and multilayered ecosystem, involving international, national, and private sector actors, all of whom interact to facilitate, regulate, and sustain the flow of goods and services across borders.
2. International organisations such as the WTO, WCO, and UNCTAD provide frameworks, standards, and platforms for cooperation that guide global trade practices.
3. National governments and trade-related agencies play a pivotal role in formulating trade policies and measures while ensuring compliance with both international obligations and national interests.
4. The private sector forms the operational backbone of international trade, where exporters and importers work alongside freight forwarders, logistics companies, banks, and insurers actively driving trade flows.
5. Trade facilitation and promotion agencies, including Chambers of Commerce and Industry Associations, act as vital intermediaries between businesses and governments, providing advocacy, information, and support for international market expansion.
6. The international trade system is deeply interconnected, meaning that disruptions in one area, whether regulatory, financial, logistical, or political, can have ripple effects across global supply chains and markets.

Notes

1 Further details about the harmonisation system will be provided in Part 4.
2 Further details about Incoterms will be provided in Part 4.
3 The UCP 600 is a set of internationally recognized rules governing L/C. In effect since July 1, 2007, UCP 600 standardises global banking practices in trade finance, providing legal certainty and operational clarity for importers, exporters, and financial institutions. It is widely adopted by banks worldwide and serves as the backbone for documentary credit transactions in international trade (ICC, 2007).
4 A more detailed examination of international dispute resolution mechanisms is provided in Part 4.

3

THE ESSENTIALS OF INTERNATIONALISATION

Learning Objectives

1 Understand internationalisation strategy and its significance from a business perspective.
2 Identify and assess the critical decision-making questions firms must address when entering foreign markets.
3 Compare different international market entry modes, understanding their advantages, disadvantages, and suitability based on strategic goals and resource capabilities.

How Internationalisation Drives Efficiency, Innovation, and Consumer Benefits

Imagine if Japanese car manufacturers like Toyota and Honda only sold their vehicles within Japan. The cost per unit would likely be much higher than what we pay today. Without the ability to spread the substantial costs of development, technology, and production facilities over a larger global market, each car would be more expensive to produce.

Internationalisation allows automobile companies to expand beyond their domestic borders into new global markets. This expansion is not just about selling more cars. It is about achieving economies of scale. By producing and selling cars in larger quantities worldwide, companies can significantly reduce the cost per unit. Operating internationally also helps firms mitigate risks

DOI: 10.4324/9781003535874-5

associated with economic downturns or political instability in a single country. If one market underperforms, a company can still stabilise its revenue through better performance in other regions. Moreover, being present in multiple markets fosters a deeper understanding of diverse consumer preferences, which can drive innovation and competitive advantage.

From a consumer perspective, internationalisation offers access to a broader selection of vehicles, competitive prices, and the latest features. Internationalisation not only drives down prices but also spurs innovation, ensuring that consumers have access to high-quality, technologically advanced vehicles.

Understanding Business Strategy, Internationalisation Strategy, and Its Significance

Before we delve into the specifics of internationalisation strategy, it is essential to first ground our understanding in the fundamentals of business strategy. At its core, business strategy is about how a firm creates, delivers, and captures value in a competitive environment. Strategy defines the company's distinctive approach to competing and the competitive advantages on which it will be based. According to Porter (1985, 1996), firms must search out areas within an industry or market where existing companies do not offer products or services. This 'white space' represents opportunities for innovation or new business development where competition is minimal or non-existent. It involves making deliberate choices about target markets, value propositions, resource allocation, and how to achieve sustainable competitive advantage. These foundational principles serve as the backbone of any strategic decision, whether operating domestically or expanding across borders.

Business strategy entails the strategic initiatives undertaken by a company to generate value for both the organisation and its stakeholders and gain a competitive advantage in the marketplace. Strategic success is typically measured through two key indicators: profitability and profit growth. Profitability refers to the return earned on invested capital, while profit growth indicates the percentage increase in net profits over a defined period.

To boost profitability and drive profit growth, firms must effectively manage the fundamental equation where profit is the difference between the price and the cost. Enhancing profitability involves either increasing the price at which goods or services are sold or reducing the costs associated with producing them. However, any price increase must be justified by the value perceived by the consumer; customers are willing to pay a higher price only if they perceive the value of the product or service to be higher than the cost.

In order to increase perceived value to justify higher prices, firms must improve the quality of products or services to provide more value to customers. Product and service differentiation – distinguishing products or services from those of competitors through unique features, design, or technological advancements – can make the offerings more appealing compared to others in the market. Moreover, enhancing the customer experience at every touchpoint can increase perceived value. This includes customer service, user experience, and overall satisfaction from purchase to post-purchase. Strong branding can enhance the perceived value of a product or service. Brands that successfully establish a reputation for reliability, prestige, or exclusivity can often price their offerings higher.[1]

Differentiation in the Airline Industry

The airline industry offers a compelling example of how firms within the same sector pursue differentiation strategies to establish a competitive edge in global markets. While all airlines operate with the core function of transporting passengers, premium carriers distinguish themselves by tailoring services that deliver unique value propositions,[2] particularly in their business class offerings.

Singapore Airlines and Qatar Airways, both rated as five-star airlines by Skytrax in 2024,[3] exemplify this strategic approach (Skytrax, 2024). Singapore Airlines has built a strong brand around luxury, privacy, and personalised service. Its business class includes lie-flat seats that convert into a full bed, with linens, duvets, and plush pillows, offering passengers direct aisle access and maximum comfort. Enhancing this experience is their 'Book the Cook' programme, which allows passengers to select gourmet meals prepared in collaboration with world-class chefs up to 24 hours before departure. The airline's iconic attention to service detail and Singaporean hospitality reinforce its premium market positioning (Singapore Airlines, n.d.).

Qatar Airways, on the other hand, innovates through its patented Qsuite, the world's first business class double bed with adjustable privacy panels, enabling passengers to create a private room on board. This is coupled with a la carte dining available at any time, award-winning luxury amenity kits, and staff trained to deliver highly personalised service (Qatar Airways, n.d.). Together, these features elevate the in-flight experience well beyond basic expectations.

Beyond the aircraft, airport lounge services have become a critical area of differentiation and customer retention. For high-value customers such as business travellers and frequent flyers, lounges are not only waiting areas but also sanctuaries for rest, productivity, and fine dining.

Singapore Airlines' SilverKris Lounges include slumberettes (dedicated sleep pods), designer interiors, and curated local cuisine. Qatar Airways' Al Mourjan Business Lounge in Doha features an expansive layout with a garden sanctuary, waterfall, private dining pods, and family-friendly amenities like a game room (Skytrax, 2024).

These premium service elements not only justify higher pricing but also drive brand loyalty and repeat business in a highly commoditised market. In the context of internationalisation, such differentiation helps airlines maintain global competitiveness, adapt to diverse customer expectations, and sustain long-term profitability.

On the other hand, if not adding more value, reducing costs can lead to an increase in profit. How can firms reduce their costs? First, operational efficiency is critical for cost optimisation. Streamlining operations to reduce waste, reduce defects, and shorten production cycle times can lower costs. Techniques such as lean manufacturing, automation, and just-in-time (JIT) system can significantly reduce production costs.

Firms can also outsource and offshore, transferring parts of the production process or services to external firms or overseas locations where costs are cheaper, or efficiency is higher. Supply chain optimisation can also help firms reduce their costs. For example, inventory management can be improved to reduce holding costs. And in some industries, economies of scale are critical for their competitive advantage. An increase in production volume spreads the fixed costs over a larger number of units, reducing the cost per unit. A larger scale can also provide bargaining power with suppliers to negotiate lower prices for raw materials.

Cost Leadership in the Airline Industry

While some airlines pursue competitive advantage through luxury and personalised services, others adopt a cost leadership strategy, focusing on efficiency, affordability, and high asset utilisation to deliver low fares and expand market share. Low-cost carriers (LCCs), such as Ryanair and AirAsia, have revolutionised air travel by minimising operating costs and maximising passenger volumes, making air transport accessible to broader segments of the population.

Ryanair, headquartered in Ireland, is one of Europe's most prominent and profitable LCCs. Its business model emphasises ultra-low fares, high aircraft utilisation, quick turnaround times, and a point-to-point route structure that avoids costly hub operations. The airline operates a single aircraft type (Boeing 737) to reduce maintenance and training costs and generates ancillary revenue through services such as baggage fees and priority boarding. Ryanair's cost leadership has delivered exceptional financial performance: in fiscal year 2023/24, the airline reported a net profit of €1.92 billion, a 34% increase over the previous year, and a total revenue of €13.44 billion (Statista, 2024; Ryanair, 2024).

In Asia, AirAsia has employed a similar model. Based in Malaysia, AirAsia focuses on no-frills services, online-only booking, and cross-border joint ventures (JVs) that enable it to operate in multiple regional markets. With subsidiaries like Thai AirAsia, Indonesia AirAsia, and AirAsia India, the airline has localised its operations while leveraging the group's centralised procurement and digital infrastructure to control costs (AirAsia, n.d.).

Both Ryanair and AirAsia demonstrate how cost leadership can be scaled globally. Their success highlights that in internationalisation, competitive advantage can stem not only from differentiation but also from the ability to deliver value through cost efficiency, particularly in price-sensitive markets.

Internationalisation Strategy and Its Benefits for Firms

Internationalisation, in the business context, is the process through which firms progressively expand their involvement in cross-border commercial activities to capitalise on opportunities in foreign markets. It involves a sequence of strategic decisions, actions, and organisational changes that enable a company to enter, operate, and grow internationally.[4]

Successful internationalisation brings significant benefits to firms. First, internationalisation provides access to new markets, allowing firms to reach more customers and scale their operations beyond domestic demand. This access can lead to a substantial increase in sales volume, particularly when firms introduce a unique product or service into an emerging or underserved market. Another important benefit is market diversification. By operating across multiple countries, firms can reduce dependence on their home market and mitigate risks related to market volatility, economic downturns, or geopolitical instability. This diversification allows companies to stabilise revenue streams, balancing losses in one region with gains in another and thus improving overall business resilience.

Uniqlo's International Growth

Fast Retailing Co., Ltd., the parent company of Uniqlo, concluded fiscal year 2024 with significantly stronger-than-expected financial results, reinforcing its position as one of the most competitive global apparel companies. The group reported a revenue of ¥2.77 trillion (approximately USD 18.78 billion[5]), marking a 20.2% year-on-year increase, and an operating profit of ¥381 billion (approximately USD 2.58 billion), up 28.2% from the previous year (Fast Retailing, 2024).

The strong performance reflects growing domestic demand in Japan and the success of Uniqlo International, with its sales increasing by 21.7% year-on-year. Fast Retailing attributes these gains to continued global demand for affordable, high-quality apparel and ongoing investments in supply chain digitalisation and retail expansion.

Retail Detail (2024) reported that the company doubled its store count in the Netherlands in 2024 by opening new locations in Rotterdam and Amsterdam, aligning with its strategic focus on strengthening its European presence. However, performance in Greater China remained subdued, with sales and profits declining due to weaker consumer sentiment, less effective marketing, and unfavourable weather conditions. The company acknowledged these challenges and indicated plans to refine its regional approach.

Companies may pursue internationalisation to access critical resources that are scarce, diverse, or cost-effective in foreign markets. These include tangible assets like natural resources, agricultural goods, or affordable labour, as well as intangible or strategic resources such as technological expertise, patents, and brand equity that can enhance a firm's long-term competitiveness. For example, to secure critical raw materials for lithium-ion batteries used in EVs and solar panels, Chinese companies are involved in at least 62 mining projects worldwide, targeting critical minerals such as lithium, cobalt, nickel, and manganese. China holds a significant share of the global supply for refining lithium and cobalt, with percentages reaching 72% and 68%, respectively, in 2022. In 2023, China manufactured over half of the EVs sold globally, possessed 60% of the world's capacity for wind turbine manufacturing, and controlled at least 80% of the solar panel supply chain at each stage of production (BBC News, 2024a; Reuters, 2025b).

Companies frequently internationalise to capitalise on more favourable regulatory environments abroad. Host countries often provide tax incentives, relaxed regulations, or trade facilitation policies to attract FDI, which can reduce operating costs and enhance competitive positioning. By strategically locating operations in markets with beneficial institutional settings, firms can optimise production and distribution, aligning with the lowest compliance costs and maximum efficiency.

From a cost-efficiency perspective, internationalisation can also enable firms to achieve economies of scale. Operating across multiple markets allows firms to increase output, thereby reducing per-unit production costs. For instance, global carmakers benefit by spreading high fixed costs (e.g. R&D, plant equipment) across large production volumes.

The following Box highlights the strategic expansion of BYD to establish its first production facility in Southeast Asia in Thailand. This expansion not only boosts BYD's capacity to serve the ASEAN market and beyond but also highlights the growing influence of Chinese EV manufacturers globally, supported by favourable government policies and increasing competitiveness in the industry.

BYD's Expansion into Thailand – Strategic Production Hub in Southeast Asia

In July 2024, BYD, China's leading EV manufacturer, inaugurated its first manufacturing plant in Southeast Asia, located in Rayong, Thailand. This marks a significant step in BYD's global expansion strategy, with the company identifying Thailand as a key gateway to the broader ASEAN region (Reuters, 2024b).

The new USD 490 million facility is designed to produce up to 150,000 vehicles per year, including both fully electric and plug-in hybrid models. It will employ approximately 10,000 workers and includes plans to assemble batteries and other core components locally. The plant is part of a broader USD 1.44 billion wave of investment by Chinese EV makers in Thailand (Reuters, 2024b).

Thailand is strategically positioned as an automotive manufacturing hub, historically dominated by Japanese brands such as Toyota and Honda. The Thai Government's EV roadmap, which targets 30% of annual vehicle production (2.5 million units) to be EVs by 2030, aligns well with BYD's investment strategy (Thailand Board of Investment, 2023). The Rayong factory will serve as BYD's ASEAN production base for regional and global markets.

In terms of market share, BYD is now Thailand's top EV brand, capturing 46% of the country's EV segment in Q1 2024 (Reuters, 2024b).

Globally, BYD's momentum has been equally notable. It overtook Tesla in Q4 2023 to become the world's largest EV seller, although Tesla reclaimed the lead in Q1 2024. Despite its international success, BYD has been operating in an increasingly saturated and competitive domestic market in China, where over 129 EV brands compete intensely in a price war. Yet, only about 20 of these firms hold a market share of 1% or more, underscoring the market's fragmentation and the difficulty of sustaining long-term profitability. Even as BYD reported a record profit of CNY 30 billion (USD 4.1 billion) in 2023, price pressures and market volatility remain central challenges in its home market (CNBC, 2025).

Decision-Making in Internationalisation

In international business, the decision-making process surrounding internationalisation involves a complex interplay of various factors, including assessing potential markets, choosing the right entry mode, determining the scale of entry, and deciding on the timing of market entry. Each of these decisions involves considering costs, risks, and strategic fit with the company's overall objectives. The decision to internationalise should be guided by thorough strategic analysis. This includes evaluating the firm's internal capabilities, industry conditions, and external market environments. Tools like Strengths, Weaknesses, Opportunities, Threats (SWOT) analysis,[6] Political, Economic, Social, Technological, Environmental, Legal (PESTEL) analysis,[7] and Porter's Five Forces can be instrumental in this process.[8]

The first and foremost question in international expansion is: which market to enter and at what scale. More favourable markets are typically those that are politically, economically, and socially stable and offer a supportive business environment. Companies should also assess the level of competition in the target market. Success is more likely in environments where the product is not yet widely available and where it can address an unmet consumer need. Timing is also critical. The advantages of entering a market early, referred to as first-mover advantages, include the ability to pre-empt rivals, establish strong brand recognition, build sales volume early, and gain cost advantages by riding down the experience curve. Additionally, early entrants may create switching costs that lock in customers, making it more difficult for later entrants to gain market share. However, first movers also face pioneering costs, the expenses that arise from navigating unfamiliar business systems, making early capital and time investments, and educating consumers about the product. These may include business failure, high promotional expenditures, and delays in achieving market acceptance.

The decision regarding how much resource to commit depends on the strategic importance of the market, expected returns, and the firm's available resources. Entering on a large scale signals strategic commitment, which can deter competitors and accelerate brand establishment, but also involves higher risk and long-term consequences. Conversely, small-scale entry allows firms to test the market with minimal risk exposure and learn about the environment before deeper commitment.[9]

Modes of International Market Entry

When firms expand internationally, one of the most critical decisions they face is choosing the appropriate entry mode. The mode of entry determines how a company establishes its presence in a foreign market and reflects strategic choices related to ownership commitment, control, risk tolerance, and resource allocation.

Wholly owned subsidiaries and JVs involve direct equity ownership and long-term capital commitment in the host country. In a wholly owned subsidiary, a firm establishes 100% ownership in a foreign entity, through either a greenfield investment or acquisition. This mode not only offers maximum control and protects proprietary assets but also entails the highest levels of risk and cost. A JV, by contrast, involves shared ownership with a local or foreign partner. JVs are beneficial for sharing costs and risks, leveraging the local partner's expertise, and meeting regulatory requirements in restricted sectors. However, JV may lead to conflicts over control, differences in strategic priorities, and the risk that proprietary technology or know-how could be unintentionally shared with the partner.

Other entry modes, such as exporting, licensing and franchising, and turnkey projects, offer lower levels of investment and risk, making them ideal for testing new markets or leveraging local partnerships. However, they typically provide limited operational control.

With exporting, firms produce goods domestically and sell them abroad, either directly or through agents and distributors. Exporting involves low risk and is often a firm's first step towards internationalisation. Downsides include exposure to tariff barriers, transportation costs, and limited market insight.

In licensing and franchising, a firm grants rights to use its intellectual property or business model in exchange for royalties. These entry modes enable rapid international expansion and help avoid barriers to investment, but they limit control over operations and increase the risk of proprietary information leakage.

In turnkey projects, firms design, construct, and operationalise a facility before handing it over to the client. This mode is often used in engineering, construction, and high-tech industries, especially in markets where firms do not plan long-term operations. The advantage lies in earning returns from specialised know-how; however, a key risk is the potential to create future competitors. By delivering a fully operational facility and transferring technical expertise, processes, and management systems to the client, the firm may inadvertently equip the client with the knowledge and capability to replicate the operations independently. Over time, the client may use these transferred capabilities to develop their own competing business.

Finally, strategic alliances are cooperative partnerships between firms, often competitors or complementary businesses, pursuing shared objectives such as market access or R&D collaboration. These alliances, which can range from JVs to shorter-term agreements, enable firms to combine complementary assets and capabilities. While alliances provide flexibility and shared learning, they also carry the risk of unintended knowledge transfer.

Selecting the appropriate mode of international market entry is a critical decision for firms seeking global expansion. This choice requires a thorough evaluation of multiple criteria to ensure alignment with the firm's strategic objectives, risk tolerance, and resource capabilities. Key areas of assessment include:

Desired level of control: Firms must decide how much control they want over foreign operations. Modes like wholly owned subsidiaries offer full control over every aspect of the business, while JVs, franchising, or licensing offers less control.

Availability of resources and costs: The choice of entry mode depends on how much capital, managerial capacity, and other resources the company is willing to commit. High-resource modes include greenfield investments, whereas exporting and licensing require less resource commitment and are less costly.

Risk tolerance: Each entry mode carries different levels of risk. Exporting is generally low-risk compared to establishing a wholly owned subsidiary. Companies need to assess their risk tolerance in terms of potential financial loss, political instability, and economic conditions of the target market.

Speed of entry: Some markets require quick entry to capitalise on opportunities or to outpace competitors. Exporting or entering into a partnership can be executed more quickly than setting up new operations from scratch. In highly competitive markets, mergers or acquisitions might provide a quicker way to establish a market presence and gain a competitive advantage.

Market knowledge: The company's familiarity with the market can influence the entry mode. If the firm has limited knowledge of the local market, partnering with a local firm through JVs or strategic alliances can provide valuable insights and reduce market entry barriers.

Long-term strategic goals and alignment with corporate strategy: The selected mode of entry should support the firm's long-term strategic objectives, such as market leadership, brand control, or technology protection.

Regulatory environment and compliance with legal requirements: Regulations such as restrictions on foreign ownership, tariffs, and non-tariff barriers can significantly impact the choice of entry mode. In some countries, foreign companies can own only up to 49% of the company. Hence, a JV with local companies is needed.

Conclusion

This chapter has explored the concept of internationalisation as a process through which firms progressively expand their involvement in cross-border commercial activities to capitalise on opportunities in foreign markets. From a business perspective, understanding internationalisation strategy is critical for firms seeking sustainable growth and competitiveness in today's globally interconnected economy. By expanding beyond domestic borders, firms can access new markets and customers, reduce costs through economies of scale, enhance innovation, and diversify risks across multiple regions.

This chapter also examined the key decision-making questions firms must address before entering foreign markets and compared the various modes of international market entry, emphasising their respective advantages, disadvantages, and alignment with strategic goals and resource capabilities.

However, as much as internationalisation offers significant opportunities, it also brings considerable complexity and uncertainty. In the next chapter, we shift the focus from opportunity to uncertainty, examining the key challenges and risks associated with internationalisation. It explores macro-level and micro-level risks. The chapter also highlights the interconnection between these risks and outlines common risk mitigation strategies employed to support international expansion.

Key Takeaway

1. Internationalisation is a process through which firms progressively expand their cross-border activities to access foreign market opportunities.
2. Benefits of internationalisation include access to new markets and customers, cost optimisation, enhanced innovation, risk diversification, and a stronger global competitive position.
3. Decision-making in internationalisation entails selecting appropriate markets by evaluating stability, competition, and unmet demand; determining the scale of entry by balancing strategic commitment with associated risks; and timing entry by weighing first-mover advantages against pioneering costs.
4. Market entry mode selection is influenced by the desired level of control, resource availability, risk tolerance, required speed of entry, market knowledge, alignment with long-term strategic objectives, and regulatory conditions in the target market.

Notes

1 For comprehensive conceptual foundations of business strategy and practical insights through applied case studies, the following texts are highly recommended:

- Hitt, M. A., Ireland, R. D., & Hoskisson, R. E. (2023). *Strategic management: Competitiveness and globalization* (14th ed.). Cengage.
- Thompson, A. A., Peteraf, M. A., Gamble, J. E., & Strickland, A. J. III. (2024). *Crafting and executing strategy: The quest for competitive advantage* (24th ed.). McGraw-Hill Education.
- Grant, R. M. (2021). *Contemporary strategy analysis* (11th ed.). Wiley.

2 A value proposition is the bundle of benefits that a firm promises to deliver to customers. When it is clearly differentiated and compelling in the eyes of the target market, it becomes a unique value proposition, a central element in positioning strategy (Kotler & Keller, 2016). In other words, 'why should a customer buy from you instead of someone else?'
3 Skytrax rating is a common benchmark of quality and services in airlines industry. Skytrax is an independent airline and airport rating organisation that is known for its comprehensive classification and evaluation system. The Skytrax rating system. The key elements of Airline Star Rating include up to 800 different areas of an airline's product and service, including front-line product quality, seats, amenities, cabin cleanliness, catering, staff service, and other service items across both airport and onboard environments. Airlines use them as benchmark and signify the quality level of each airline's product and service standards. Further information can be found at https://skytraxratings.com/
4 For a thorough overview of internationalisation and global strategy, how firms design and implement strategies to compete in an increasingly complex and interconnected international environment. The following texts provide valuable insights and frameworks:
   - Lasserre, P., & Monteiro, F. (2022). *Global strategic management* (5th ed.). Bloomsbury Publishing.
   - Peng, M. W., & Meyer, K. E. (2023). *Global strategy* (5th ed.). Cengage.
5 USD figures are based on an average 2024 exchange rate of 1 USD = 147.5 JPY.
6 At the firm level, SWOT analysis helps identify a company's strengths and weaknesses in relation to its internal resources, while highlighting opportunities and threats in the external environment.
7 PESTEL is a useful external macro-environmental analysis framework. It evaluates political, economic, social, technological, environmental, and legal factors within a target country. By systematically analysing these dimensions, firms can anticipate potential market barriers, such as restrictive trade policies, sociocultural differences, or technological infrastructure gaps that may affect market entry and operations.
8 At the industry level, Porter's Five Forces framework examines the competitive structure of the target market by analysing the threat of new entrants, bargaining power of buyers and suppliers, intensity of rivalry, and threat of substitutes (Porter, 1985). This analysis helps firms determine the attractiveness of the industry in the host country and the likely profitability of international expansion.
9 For a solid grounding in the conceptual foundations of decision-making in internationalisation, and modes of international market entry, see
   - Hill, C. W. L. (2023). *International business: Competing in the global marketplace* (14th ed.). McGraw-Hill Education.
   - Cavusgil, S. T., Knight, G., & Riesenberger, J. R. (2021). *International business: The new realities* (5th ed.). Pearson.
   - Daniels, J. D., Radebaugh, L. H., & Sullivan, D. P. (2021). *International business: Environments and operations* (17th ed.). Pearson.
   - Verbeke, A., & Lee, I. (2022). *International business strategy: Rethinking the foundations of global corporate success* (2nd ed.). Cambridge University Press.

4

INTERNATIONALISATION

Key Issues and Challenges

Learning Objectives

1. Understand macro-level and micro-level risks associated with internationalisation.
2. Recognise the interconnected nature of risks and how cascading disruptions can amplify operational challenges.
3. Examine commonly adopted risk mitigation strategies in managing uncertainty in international business.

The Complex Voyage of Global Business Expansion

Expanding a business internationally is much like sailing into open waters. For firms, internationalisation offers the potential to reach new customers, form strategic alliances, and optimise operations across borders. The promise of reaching new customers, new business partners, and reducing costs by expanding operations overseas can be very appealing.

Yet the voyage is not without its risks. The international business environment is filled with unpredictable currents, ranging from legal complexity, cultural misalignment, and economic turbulence. For instance, Google continuously adjusts its operations to comply with Europe's stringent privacy laws under the General Data Protection Regulation (GDPR), which differ from US standards[1]. Walmart's unsuccessful expansion into Germany also serves as a

DOI: 10.4324/9781003535874-6

cautionary example. Despite its global dominance, the retailer failed to align with local consumer preferences and labour practices, ultimately resulting in its market exit[2]. Likewise, firms operating in politically or economically unstable markets can face sudden currency fluctuations, policy reversals, or regulatory overhauls, which can significantly disrupt operations and profitability. For example, the Turkish lira has experienced significant volatility in recent years, attributed to economic policies, high inflation rates, and political uncertainties[3]. For businesses, such volatility poses substantial transaction and economic risks.

Sailing into international markets demands both preparation and agility. Businesses that successfully navigate these global waters are not merely lucky nor do they succeed by chance; rather, they succeed by being well-informed, adaptable, and strategically prepared.

Global trade offers significant opportunities for businesses to expand and prosper, but it also presents a variety of challenges that can complicate operations and strategy. Expanding business operations internationally can expose a company to a range of risks that vary in scale, scope, and controllability.

Macro-level risks are systemic and often uncontrollable external disruptions. These include geopolitical tensions, political instability, economic volatility, natural disasters, and technological disruption. These risks originate outside the firm's immediate environment and typically impact entire industries or regions. Frameworks such as PESTEL analysis, which evaluates political, economic, social, technological, environmental, and legal factors, are widely employed to assess such an external business environment.[4] In contrast, micro-level risks are internal to the firm or arise from the specific contexts in which it operates internationally. These include business risks, operational failures, supply chain breakdowns, or regulatory non-compliance.

It is essential to recognise that crises such as geopolitical conflicts, economic shocks, regulatory uncertainty, and others are often interconnected, with one frequently exacerbating the effects of another. Likewise, there is significant interdependence between macro-level risks (systemic and external) and micro-level risks (firm-specific and operational). For example, a macro-level disruption, like a global pandemic or a trade embargo, can quickly evolve into a micro-level crisis by impeding supply chains, restricting access to critical resources, or shifting consumer demand patterns in key markets. As a result, effective internationalisation demands a holistic risk management approach, integrating assessments of both external systemic threats and internal operational vulnerabilities.

Macro-Level Risks

Political risk: This may arise from geopolitical tensions, political conflicts, wars, governmental instability, changes in government, civil unrest, or more drastic political disruptions, which can disrupt supply chains and business operations. Such political shifts often lead to regulatory changes that directly affect market dynamics. For example, new governments may revise laws to reflect shifting national priorities or introduce retaliatory measures such as trade restrictions or economic sanctions, which further reshape market conditions and hinder market access. Thus, political change and regulatory change are closely intertwined, with political instability frequently triggering regulatory uncertainty that increases operational risks for international firms.

For example, the Russia–Ukraine war, which began in February 2022, has significantly disrupted global trade flows, particularly in energy, agriculture, and fertilisers, and caused a shift in global supply chain structures. According to the OECD (2023), the conflict disrupted grain exports from Ukraine, one of the world's largest wheat and sunflower oil producers, resulting in volatile food prices and inflation spikes globally.[5] On the energy front, Europe was most affected due to its dependency on Russian gas. Sanctions and retaliatory export restrictions from Russia led to a global scramble for liquefied natural gas (LNG) with ripple effects on fuel and manufacturing costs worldwide (Van de Graaf, 2023). Additionally, the war also disrupted shipping routes in the Black Sea. Businesses had to find alternate routes or face rising shipping premiums (UNCTAD, 2024a; German Economic Team, 2024).

Economic risk: This could arise from political and macroeconomic instability, inflation, currency fluctuations, economic recessions, or financial crises, all of which can impact firms' operational stability and financial performance. For example, on May 31, 2023, the Turkish lira experienced a significant surge in volatility, with the 1-year volatility gauge rising to 45.46%, its highest level in at least 15 years. The situation illustrated the intersection of political and economic risk, where leadership transitions and perceived policy unpredictability can significantly impact investor confidence, exchange rate stability, and financial market behaviour, especially in emerging markets (Reuters, 2023).

Tariffs, Trade, and Turbulence

The ongoing impacts of trade tensions between major economies, such as the United States and China, including tariffs, sanctions, and countermeasures, continue to shape global trade dynamics. During President Trump's first administration, the United States imposed significant tariffs on Chinese goods in 2018, citing unfair trade practices and intellectual property theft, which led China to retaliate with tariffs on American products (Bown, 2021). This tit-for-tat escalation affected billions of dollars in goods, disrupting global supply chains, increasing costs for consumers and businesses. The consequences extended far beyond trade balances, shaking investor confidence and rattling financial markets. Following major tariff announcements in June 2018, the S&P 500 experienced immediate sell-offs. On August 23, 2019, after Trump tweeted about retaliatory tariffs, the Dow Jones fell by over 600 points in a single day (Davis, 2019). The FX markets also responded sharply. The Chinese yuan depreciated beyond the psychologically critical level of 7 CNY/USD in August 2019, its weakest point in over a decade (Chen et al., 2023).

On April 2, 2025, under President Trump's second administration, a sweeping 10% tariff on all imports was announced, effective April 5, along with a 104% tariff on Chinese goods. The global economic response was immediate and severe. A total of $10 trillion in global equity value was erased in three trading days, the worst market wipeout since the COVID-19 crash. The S&P 500 dropped 10% in two days, while the Dow Jones and Nasdaq also suffered heavy losses. The Chinese yuan hit a 19-month low at 7.2038 per USD (Chughtai & Haddad, 2025)

The trade tensions between the United States and China vividly illustrate how macro-level risks, such as protectionist policies and geopolitical shifts, can cascade into micro-level consequences that directly affect firms, investors, and consumers. The imposition of tariffs under both Trump administrations represents a form of systemic external disruption – policy-driven, politically motivated, and largely uncontrollable at the firm level. However, their effects quickly permeated operational realities: businesses faced higher input costs, restructured supply chains, and currency-related pricing volatility. Financial markets responded with sharp sell-offs and heightened uncertainty.

Legal risk: Navigating different legal environments and meeting compliance and regulatory standards across different countries can be challenging. Each country has its own set of laws and regulations governing business operations, which can vary significantly. For example, the European Union's GDPR, enacted in 2018, was established to harmonise data privacy laws across Europe, granting individuals greater control over their personal data and imposing strict obligations on organisations handling such data. Notably, the regulation has extraterritorial reach, meaning it applies to any company processing the personal data of EU residents, regardless of the company's location. Non-compliance can result in fines of up to €20 million or 4% of a company's global annual turnover, whichever is higher (Houser & Voss, 2018).

In 2019, France's data protection authority, CNIL, fined Google €50 million for lacking transparency and valid consent in personalised advertising practices. CNIL found that Google did not provide users with clear information on data processing and failed to obtain proper consent for ad personalisation (Fortra, 2019). In 2023, the Irish Data Protection Commission imposed a €1.2 billion fine on Facebook (Meta Platforms Ireland Limited) for transferring personal data of European users to the United States without adequate safeguards, violating GDPR provisions on international data transfers (European Data Protection Board, 2023).

Technological risk: The exponential growth of e-commerce and digital trade raises questions about regulations, cross-border data flows, privacy, and security. Advances in technology, such as blockchain, artificial intelligence, and the Internet of Things are revolutionising trade logistics and compliance but also present challenges in terms of cybersecurity and digital divides between countries. High-profile cyberattacks have revealed the vulnerability of digital infrastructure. In 2024, ransomware attacks on Indian companies caused widespread operational delays and financial losses (Deutsche Welle, 2024). In July 2024, a global IT outage caused by a faulty CrowdStrike update affected thousands of companies and grounded flights at major airports, including London Heathrow, Sydney, and Frankfurt. The BBC reported system crashes in sectors from retail to banking, illustrating the systemic risk of third-party software dependency (BBC News, 2024b; CNN, 2024).

A recent example illustrating the profound impact of technological risks on business is the widespread power outage that disrupted large parts of Spain and Portugal on April 28, 2025, halting operations, interrupting supply chains, and causing significant financial losses for many firms. The blackout brought critical transportation systems, public services, and commercial operations to a standstill. Notably, Madrid's Barajas International Airport and Lisbon's Humberto Delgado Airport were forced to close due to a complete loss of power, while telecommunication services were interrupted across both countries. Urban metro systems in Madrid and Lisbon were also affected, with passengers trapped in trains stalled between stations. Healthcare services experienced significant disruptions as well, with major hospitals in Madrid and multiple Portuguese medical facilities cancelling scheduled surgeries due to power-related complications (Euronews, 2025; Al Jazeera, 2025; BBC News, 2025).

Environmental risk: Lately, this has emerged as one of the most unpredictable and destabilising risks in international trade. No longer rare anomalies, extreme weather, climate events, and natural disasters are now regular disruptors of global supply chains. In the context of internationalisation, these events represent a growing source of operational risk, as they often strike without warning and cause widespread disruption across multiple regions and industries.

For example, in late 2011, Thailand experienced its worst flooding in over five decades, with severe consequences not only for the local but also for global technology supply chains. The floodwaters swamped seven major industrial estates. Thailand at the time accounted for nearly 45% of the world's hard disk drive (HDD) production, making it the second-largest HDD exporter globally. Major suppliers, including Western Digital, Toshiba, and Seagate, had production facilities in the flood-affected zones (The Guardian, 2011a).

This led to a global shortage of hard drives, with prices rising by more than 150% in just a few months. The crisis highlighted the vulnerability of global supply chains that rely on highly concentrated manufacturing regions. As BBC News (2011) reported, computer manufacturers such as HP and Dell warned of supply constraints that would impact personal computer production well into 2012. The shortage significantly delayed laptop and server manufacturing, especially during the holiday retail season.

Another notable example is the Tōhoku earthquake and tsunami, which struck Japan on March 11, 2011. Measuring magnitude 9.0, the most powerful earthquake ever recorded in Japan, it occurred off the north-eastern coast of Honshu, triggering a massive tsunami with waves reaching up to 40.5 metres. The disaster claimed over 15,000 lives and destroyed entire towns. It also caused a meltdown at the Fukushima Daiichi Nuclear Power Plant, resulting in the worst nuclear accident since Chernobyl (National Geographic Education, n.d.; NHK World-Japan, 2025). As a major hub in global supply chains, particularly for automotive, electronics, and semiconductor components, Japan experienced widespread industrial shutdowns. Toyota, Honda, and Nissan were forced to suspend production due to infrastructure damage and parts shortages. Key ports such as Sendai and Hitachinaka were also damaged, disrupting maritime shipping and container logistics. These cascading effects sent shockwaves through the global economy, delaying automotive production worldwide and exposing the vulnerabilities of JIT inventory systems (Teh et al., 2011; The Guardian, 2011b).

Micro-Level Risks

At the micro level, risks are internal to the firm or arise from the specific contexts in which it operates internationally. These include business risks, operational failures, supply chain breakdowns, or regulatory non-compliance, which may arise either from internal factors within firms or as impacts from macro-level factors.

Business risks: Business risks associated with internationalisation are multifaceted and often stem from challenges in understanding and adapting to foreign market conditions. A product or service that performs well in one country may fail in another due to variations in consumer behaviour, cultural norms, and brand perception. Misjudging market demand or overestimating the size and purchasing power of the target segment can result in excess inventory, weak sales, and under-utilised resources. In many cases, firms must also contend with heightened competition from both local incumbents and other international entrants, which may already possess deep insights into the market and established consumer loyalty. Moreover, inadequate market knowledge, such as a poor grasp of local preferences, regulatory frameworks, or distribution structures, can significantly impede business performance.

To mitigate such risks, firms should undertake comprehensive market research prior to entry and maintain a practice of continuous environmental scanning to monitor shifts in trends, consumer expectations, and competitive forces. Successful internationalisation requires firms to regularly reassess and adapt their strategies in response to evolving external conditions and internal performance.

Moreover, internationalisation has brought firms substantial compliance and *legal risk*, which includes the failure to adhere to local laws, international regulations, industry standards, contractual obligations, or dispute resolution mechanisms. Non-compliance can lead to fines, legal sanctions, reputational damage, or even operational shutdowns.

Operational risk: With regard to operational risk, firms are exposed to risks stemming from system failures, human errors, supply chain disruptions, quality control issues, and unreliable suppliers. Timely and consistent delivery of goods is critical in international markets, where reputational and financial costs of delays can be amplified across borders. For instance, the COVID-19 pandemic severely disrupted global logistics systems. Lockdowns, labour shortages, and travel restrictions resulted in widespread port congestion, delayed shipments, and drastically increased lead times across industries (National Bureau of Economic Research, 2024). Another notable example of infrastructural vulnerability occurred in March 2021, when the container ship *Ever Given* ran aground in the Suez Canal, obstructing one of the world's busiest maritime routes. The six-day blockage held up over 400 vessels, disrupting a shipping route that handles approximately 12% of global trade (BBC News, 2021).

Financial and payment risks: These are central concerns in international trade, as they directly affect a firm's cash flow, profitability, and overall liquidity position. Financial risk broadly refers to the potential for losses due to fluctuations in interest rates, exchange rates, credit availability, or the firm's liquidity position. Payment risk is particularly relevant in cross-border transactions and involves the possibility that one party will fail to make full payment on time or in the agreed currency. This can arise due to a range of factors, including late payments, defaults, or currency devaluation.

Payment risk is closely linked to credit risk, particularly in open account or delayed-payment arrangements. It may stem from counterparty insolvency, bankruptcy, deliberate fraud, or be exacerbated by political instability, currency controls, or government-imposed restrictions that prevent payment completion. On the operational side, documentation errors, such as discrepancies in shipping or customs paperwork, can delay or nullify payments, especially in cases where instruments like L/C or documentary collection (D/C) are used. In addition, foreign exchange volatility also heightens a significant role in financial exposure. For instance, a sharp depreciation of a buyer's local currency can make an international settlement unaffordable. Therefore, international firms must adopt risk mitigation tools such as hedging, trade credit insurance, or secure payment terms to manage exposure and ensure financial stability across borders.

Risk Mitigation in International Trade

In the global trading system, risks exist at both macro and micro levels. Managing risk in international trade requires an integrated, multilayered approach. While micro-level risks are often manageable through firm-level strategies and financial tools, macro-level risks are more difficult to control or predict due to their dependence on external forces such as geopolitics or regulatory change. As such, continuous monitoring and evaluation of the business environment, through tools such as country risk assessments, scenario planning, and policy tracking, are essential components of a sound internationalisation strategy.

At the micro level, firms encounter a range of operational and financial risks that require proactive management. Business risk refers to internal vulnerabilities such as supply chain disruptions, labour shortages, or managerial inefficiencies. To address these challenges, firms may adopt agile operations and flexible sourcing strategies, with a growing emphasis on reshoring and nearshoring, bringing production closer to home or to politically stable regions to reduce exposure. Additionally, firms are increasingly adopting supply chain diversification strategies, forming partnerships across multiple geographic regions to minimise dependency on a single source and increase resilience in the face of future shocks (UNCTAD, 2024b). For example, Apple's recent expansion of production in India reflects a strategy to reduce dependency on China and mitigate geopolitical risks (BBC News, 2022), and Tesla brings its lithium iron phosphate battery supply chain to the United States to reduce its dependency on Chinese suppliers (Reuters, 2024a).

At the firm level, legal risk encompasses issues such as contractual disputes, non-compliance with foreign regulations, and liability exposure. These risks are commonly mitigated through thorough country-specific legal risk assessments, consultation with international legal experts, and careful selection of reliable business partners. Additionally, embedding clear terms and conditions and dispute resolution clauses (including choice of law and jurisdiction) into contracts helps ensure enforceability and reduces uncertainty across multiple jurisdictions.

Financial and payment risk – such as non-payment, delayed payments, or buyer insolvency – is another significant concern in international trade. Firms mitigate these risks through trade finance instruments, including L/C, documentary collections (D/Cs), and export credit insurance. Depending on the risk profile of their trading partners, exporters may also require advance payments. Conducting thorough credit checks further reduces exposure to default risk. In addition, to manage currency fluctuations, firms can use financial instruments such as forward contracts, currency options, and swaps, often arranged through financial institutions.

Beyond technical tools, strategic relationship management is essential to minimise business risks. Carefully selecting reliable business partners is a critical first step. Firms should assess potential buyers, suppliers, and logistics providers based not only on pricing and service offerings but also on their professionalism, financial stability, and track record. This due diligence can be conducted through credible sources such as industry associations, chambers of commerce, credit rating agencies, and references from existing clients or long-standing partners. Such rigorous vetting reduces the likelihood of disputes, non-performance, or unethical practices that could disrupt operations.[6]

Conclusion

Although internationalisation can significantly benefit firms in many ways, it inevitably exposes them to a wide range of risks arising from the complexities of diverse political, economic, legal, technological, and cultural environments. This chapter has highlighted macro-level systemic risks, such as political instability, economic volatility, regulatory changes, technological disruptions, and environmental risks, as well as micro-level firm-specific risks, including operational, financial, and legal challenges. It emphasised that these risks are highly interconnected, with systemic events often cascading into firm-level crises, amplifying business and operational vulnerabilities. In this context, effective risk management is not a peripheral activity but a central element of international business strategy, enabling firms to build resilience and maintain competitiveness amid global uncertainties. Through proactive risk identification, rigorous due diligence, careful partner selection, and the adoption of financial, legal, and operational mitigation tools, firms can navigate uncertainty while safeguarding long-term growth.

The subsequent part of this book further examines why international trade matters for countries. It begins by discussing the economic significance of international trade, its relationship with GDP. It then provides an overview of major traded products, trade values, and leading players in global trade. It then explores International Trade's Ideologies and Theoretical Compass by, tracing key trade theories and explaining how these have shaped trade ideologies, policies, and regulatory frameworks. Finally, it examines International Trade Policies and Measures, focusing on why governments implement trade measures, the diverse mechanisms used to regulate global trade, and the role of regional economic integration in shaping trade flows.

Key Takeaway

1 Internationalisation offers firms growth, diversification, and competitive advantage, but also exposes them to geopolitical and economic instability, regulatory complexity, operational disruptions, financial risks, and cultural challenges.
2 Macro-level risks are systemic and external, including geopolitical instability, economic volatility, regulatory shifts, natural disasters, and technological failures. These are largely beyond a firm's direct control.
3 Micro-level risks are firm-specific and operational, such as supply chain breakdowns, compliance failures, contractual disputes, and financial or payment risks.
4 Macro and micro risks are highly interconnected. Systemic shocks, such as wars, pandemics, or global financial crises, can cascade into firm-level disruptions, amplifying operational vulnerabilities.
5 Effective internationalisation demands a comprehensive and integrated approach to risk management. Firms must carry out thorough risk assessments, implement appropriate mitigation strategies, rigorously evaluate and select trustworthy business partners, and foster long-term partnerships.

Notes

1 Google has been under scrutiny in the European Union for various issues including antitrust violations and data privacy concerns. The EU's General Data Protection Regulation (GDPR) has significantly impacted how Google and other tech companies handle user data in Europe. This has led to various legal challenges and fines for non-compliance. For example, Google was fined €50 million by the French Commission Nationale de l'Informatique et des Libertés (CNIL) for not having a valid legal basis to process the personal data of its users, particularly in relation to ad personalisation. This was due to a lack of transparency and inadequate information, as well as not obtaining users' consent in a sufficiently informed and unambiguous manner (CNIL, 2019). Also, Google was fined €600,000 by the Belgian Data Protection Authority for not respecting a Belgian citizen's right to be forgotten. The fine was imposed due to Google's refusal to delist certain links containing outdated or unsubstantiated information that could damage the citizen's reputation, coupled with a lack of transparency in their delisting procedures (EDPB, 2020).

2 Walmart entered the German market in 1997 but withdrew in 2006 due to various challenges. These included cultural misfits, such as the German market's unfamiliarity with Walmart's low-price strategy, and operational challenges like the difficulty in modifying store formats and management styles to better suit local tastes (Landler & Barboza, 2006).
3 In May 2023, the Turkish Lira experienced a significant surge in implied volatility, with the 1-year volatility gauge rising to 45.46%, its highest level in at least 15 years (Reuters, 2023).
4 For a detailed discussion on PESTEL analysis, see
   - Johnson, G., Scholes, K., & Whittington, R. (2020). *Exploring strategy: Text and cases* (12th ed.). Pearson;
   - Wheelen, T. L., & Hunger, J. D. (2017). *Strategic management and business policy: Globalization, innovation, and sustainability* (15th ed.). Pearson; and
   - Grant, R. M. (2021). *Contemporary strategy analysis* (11th ed.). Wiley.
5 Ukraine's exports are dominated by corn, seed oils, wheat, iron ore, and soybeans. Key destinations for the exports are Poland, Romania, Türkiye, China, and Germany. The country's imports are dominated by refined petroleum, cars, petroleum gas, packaged medicaments, and explosive ammunition. Key sources of these imports are Poland, China, Germany, Türkiye, and United States (OEC, n.d.-i, https://oec.world/en/profile/country/ukr).

   The top exports of Russia are crude petroleum, refined petroleum, petroleum gas, coal briquettes, and gold. The top export destinations are China, India, Türkiye, Kazakhstan, and Brazil. Russia is the world's largest exporter of wheat, semi-finished iron, nitrogenous fertilizers, non-fillet frozen fish, and nuclear reactors. The top imports of Russia are cars, packaged medicines, broadcasting equipment, tractors, and computers. The top sources of imports are China, Türkiye, Germany, Kazakhstan, and Italy (OEC, n.d.-f, https://oec.world/en/profile/country/rus).
6 In Japan, for example, careful partner selection is deeply embedded in business culture. *Nemawashi* refers to the informal process of building consensus and trust before formal decision-making or partnership agreements. Firms often conduct extensive relationship-building activities to understand a potential partner's reputation, values, and reliability before formalising any agreements. Japanese companies also place high importance on long-term trust and compatibility, often consulting trade associations, local business networks, and existing clients to validate a partner's credibility. For further details, see De Mente, B. L. (2014). *Japan's cultural code words: 233 key terms that explain the attitudes and behavior of the Japanese.* Tuttle Publishing.

   A study on trust-building among international SMEs by Udomkit et al. (2020) also highlights the importance of trust in cross-border business. Competence and professionalism are fundamental to establishing reliable business relationships. By demonstrating expertise and consistently fulfilling commitments, firms reassure their partners of both reliability and capability. Business relationships are further reinforced through honesty and integrity, as ethical behaviour, transparency, and honouring commitments contribute to a strong foundation of trust. Empathy and genuine care also play a vital role. Understanding and responding to a partner's needs with sincerity fosters mutual respect and a deeper sense of connection. When these three components of competence, integrity, and empathy are consistently upheld, they cultivate trust and resilient partnerships that can withstand challenges and support long-term collaboration.

PART 3

Why Does International Trade Matter for Countries?

5

THE ECONOMIC SIGNIFICANCE OF INTERNATIONAL TRADE

Learning Objectives

1 Recognise the significance of international trade as a key driver of national economic growth.
2 Understand key trade indicators, leading players in global trade, and major traded products.

How Much Does Your Economy Rely on International Trade?

Have you ever considered how dependent your country is on international trade?

One of the most commonly used indicators of a nation's openness to the global economy is the Trade-to-GDP ratio. This metric measures the combined value of exports and imports as a percentage of a country's GDP. A higher ratio signifies deeper integration into global trade networks and a greater level of economic dependence on international markets.

Some of the world's most prosperous and dynamic economies are also among the most trade-dependent. For example, in 2024, Luxembourg's trade-to-GDP ratio exceeds 398%, Singapore's is around 322%, Ireland surpasses 253%, and the United Arab Emirates exceeds 202%. Similarly, countries such as Belgium, Vietnam, the Netherlands, and Malaysia maintain exceptionally high trade-to-GDP ratios, underscoring their strong reliance on cross-border trade (World Bank Group, n.d.-e).

DOI: 10.4324/9781003535874-8

The Economic Significance of International Trade

Trade is a foundational economic activity that has shaped human societies and underpinned the development of civilisations throughout history (International Trade Council, 2023). In ancient times, civilisations such as the Egyptians, Sumerians, Greeks, and Romans engaged in cross-regional trade involving commodities like grain, spices, textiles, and precious metals. One of the most notable early trade networks was the Silk Road, which emerged during China's Han Dynasty (206 BCE to 220 CE). Spanning more than 6,000 miles, this network facilitated commercial and cultural exchanges between Asia, Europe, and Africa.[1]

The period from the fifteenth to the seventeenth century, known as the Age of Exploration, marked a turning point in global trade. Driven by the desire to bypass Ottoman and Venetian control of traditional trade routes, European nations sought direct maritime access to Asia's valuable spices, silk, porcelain, and other luxury goods. European explorers such as Christopher Columbus, Vasco da Gama, and Ferdinand Magellan pioneered oceanic navigation in pursuit of these economic opportunities. These expeditions led to the establishment of global trade routes and colonial outposts, facilitating the exchange of goods, resources, and cultural influences among continents. Subsequently, the Age of Colonisation saw European powers expand their influence across the Americas, Africa, and Asia. Colonisation significantly reshaped international trade by opening new markets and securing sources of raw materials. The establishment of powerful trading entities such as the British East India Company, founded in 1600, illustrates the increasing scale and organisation of global commerce during this era (Bernstein, 2008; International Trade Council, 2023).

The late eighteenth and nineteenth centuries witnessed the Industrial Revolution. Technological innovations, including the steam engine, and enhanced transportation infrastructure, enabled mass production and broadened the scale of international trade. Communication breakthroughs such as the telegraph improved coordination across distances, further accelerating the pace and complexity of global commerce.

However, in the twentieth century, World War I (1914–1918) devastated economies and trade networks, and the subsequent Great Depression further constrained global economic activity. World War II (1939–1945) compounded these challenges. In the post-war period, nations recognised the need for structured cooperation to stabilise and liberalise trade. As a result, major institutions were created, including the IMF and the World Bank, to support financial stability and development. In 1948, the General Agreement on Tariffs and Trade (GATT) was established to reduce trade barriers and promote free trade. GATT later evolved into the WTO in 1995, which now serves as the central body governing international trade rules (International Trade Council, 2023; World Trade Organization (WTO), n.d.-c).

In recent decades, the digital revolution has transformed the landscape of international trade. The rapid advancement of the internet, digital technologies, and e-commerce platforms has empowered firms of all sizes to conduct cross-border transactions with remarkable speed and efficiency. Global supply chains have become highly integrated, optimising the production, distribution, and consumption of goods across multiple countries. This digital shift has redefined the pace and nature of international trade, emphasising speed, connectivity, and information-driven value creation.[2]

International Trade's Contribution to GDP

Throughout history, international trade has served as a powerful engine of economic development. Therefore, economic and trade policies do not operate in isolation; they are deeply interconnected, with decisions in one sphere often influencing outcomes in the other. To fully grasp the economic significance of trade, it is essential to examine how it contributes to national economic performance.

In economics, one of the key economic indicators used to measure the economic performance of a country is GDP. GDP is a broad measure of a nation's overall economic activity and is commonly used as a standard metric for gauging the size of an economy of a country and to compare economic activity across countries, as well as its growth rate.[3] GDP can be measured using three primary methods: the expenditure (or spending) approach, the output (or production) approach, and the income approach. Among these, the expenditure approach is the most widely used. It calculates GDP based on the total expenditure by various economic agents within the economy by aggregating the spending of households, businesses, government, and net exports, and is expressed through the following formula:

$$GDP = C + G + I + NX,$$

where C = consumption; G = government spending; I = investment; NX = net exports.

Consumption refers to private consumption expenditures by households on goods and services. It encompasses everyday spending on items such as food, clothing, healthcare, and entertainment.

Government spending includes government consumption expenditure and investment, such as investment in public infrastructure, equipment, and salaries. During periods of economic downturn, government spending often plays a prominent role in sustaining GDP when private consumption and business investment decline.

Investment represents private investment, including business expenditures on capital goods such as machinery, equipment, and infrastructure. Investment is a vital component of GDP, as it enhances an economy's productive capacity and contributes to jobs.

Net exports are calculated as the value of a country's total exports minus its total imports (NX = exports – imports). A positive net export figure indicates a trade surplus, while a negative value signals a trade deficit.

According to the World Bank, the world's GDP has drastically increased, moving from just USD 1.36 trillion in 1960 to USD 111.33 trillion in 2024. In 2023, the world's largest economies were led by the United States, China, Germany, Japan, and India. The United States remained the top economy with a nominal GDP of approximately USD 27.72 trillion, representing 26.1% of global output. Its GDP per capita stood at USD 80,706, supported by a growth rate of 2.89%.

China ranked second, contributing USD 17.79 trillion (16.76% of global GDP), with a GDP per capita of USD 12,509 and an annual growth rate of 5.25%. Germany overtook Japan as the third largest economy, posting USD 4.53 trillion (4.26% of global GDP) with GDP per capita at USD 53,528. Japan followed with USD 4.20 trillion (3.96% of global GDP) and a GDP per capita of USD 33,806, while India ranked fifth with USD 3.57 trillion, recording the highest growth rate among the top ten (8.15%), though its GDP per capita remained relatively low at USD 2,481 due to its large population base.[4]

Global Leaders in International Trade

According to the latest data from United Nations Conference on Trade and Development (UNCTAD) (2024c), China, the United States, and Germany are the top three countries by total trade value. China leads the world in trade, with a trade value of approximately USD 6.0 trillion, comprising about USD 3.4 trillion in exports and USD 2.6 trillion in imports. This performance is largely underpinned by China's dominant role in global manufacturing, electronics, and machinery exports. The United States follows closely with a trade value of around USD 5.3 trillion, reflecting its large import base (USD 3.2 trillion) alongside strong exports in high-value sectors such as aircraft, pharmaceuticals, and services. Germany, recognised for its industrial and export-oriented economy, ranks third, with a trade value nearing USD 3.3 trillion, driven by automobiles, chemical products, and machinery exports.

Other major trading nations include the Netherlands, a key European logistics hub with USD 1.87 trillion in trade, and Japan, with around USD 1.53 trillion, reflecting its continued strength in the automobile and electronics sectors. South Korea, France, Italy, Hong Kong SAR, and the United Kingdom round out the top ten, each with trade values exceeding USD 1.2 trillion.

Trade Openness

'Trade openness index' or 'Trade-to-GDP ratio' is an indicator used to assess how open a country is to international trade. It reflects the degree to which a country engages in imports and exports relative to its overall economic activity, typically measured as a percentage of GDP. Globally, the trade openness index varies significantly, but most countries have an index ranging from 50% to 100%. Singapore is renowned for its exceptionally high level of trade openness, often exceeding 300%, indicating that its economy is heavily reliant on trade. This extraordinary level of openness can be attributed to the country's strong commitment to free trade, with minimal barriers to import and export activities. In comparison to the United States and China, despite being major players in international trade, the United States has a relatively low Trade Openness Index, typically around 25% to 30%, whereas China's trade openness has evolved substantially alongside its economic growth and restructuring. China's trade openness index rose from just 4.8% in 1970 to over 60% during its peak between 2005 and 2008, and it currently stands at approximately 40% (Our World in Data, n.d.).[5]

The Balance of Trade

The balance of trade (BOT) refers to the difference between the value of a country's exports and the value of its imports over a specific period. When a country imports more than it exports, it experiences a trade deficit. Conversely, when a country exports more than it imports, it records a trade surplus. A trade surplus can contribute positively to a nation's GDP, while a trade deficit may exert downward pressure on GDP.

The statistic from UNCTAD[6] shows that in 2024, the country with the highest merchandise trade deficit was the United States, with approximately USD 1.31 trillion, whereas China had the highest trade surplus, with approximately USD 991.7 billion. This surplus reflects its manufacturing prowess, competitive pricing, and extensive global supply chain integration. Germany, long recognised as Europe's economic powerhouse, also maintains a substantial trade surplus of approximately USD 259.9 billion, supported by its robust industrial base and exports of capital goods. Russia recorded a notable surplus USD 132.9, largely attributed to its exports of oil, gas, and other natural resources, though recent geopolitical sanctions have impacted its trade dynamics.

Other significant trade surplus economies include Norway, which benefits from energy exports; Switzerland, which is known for its high-value goods such as pharmaceuticals and precision instruments; and Ireland, which hosts many MNCs in the pharmaceutical and tech sectors. South Korea, Singapore, and Vietnam also enjoy trade surpluses due to their strong positions in electronics, shipping, and labour-intensive manufacturing. These surpluses reflect competitive advantages in specific sectors, efficient production ecosystems, and sustained foreign demand.

Conversely, trade deficits arise when a country imports more than it exports, often reflecting high domestic consumption, weak export capacity, or dependency on foreign goods. The United States holds the world's largest trade deficit, estimated at approximately USD 1.31 trillion.[7] This persistent deficit reflects the role of the United States as a global consumer market, a strong dollar, and ongoing demand for foreign goods, especially electronics and consumer products. India ranks second, with a trade deficit of around USD 275.5 billion, primarily due to heavy reliance on imports of crude oil, gold, and electronic components. Other major countries with significant trade deficits include Japan, the Philippines, France, Ukraine, the United Kingdom, Mexico, and Türkiye.

In general, a trade surplus is often perceived as a positive indicator of economic strength, while a trade deficit is typically viewed as a negative sign. However, this interpretation is oversimplified. The BOT, on its own, is not a definitive measure of a country's economic health. It must be assessed alongside other indicators, such as GDP growth, investment levels, employment rates, and the overall business cycle. Excessive reliance on foreign demand can expose an economy to external shocks. Additionally, large trade surpluses can lead to geopolitical frictions. For example, China's persistent and substantial trade surplus has been a central issue in US trade policy discussions and has triggered a wave of tariffs and countermeasures in recent years. Conversely, some high-performing economies, such as the United States and the United Kingdom, have maintained long-standing trade deficits while continuing to play leading roles in the global economy.

Conclusion

This chapter has explored the economic significance of international trade from past to present. It highlights the critical role of international trade in shaping national economies and examines the key players that influence global trade flows. The discussion further examines the relationship between trade performance and key economic indicators, including GDP, trade balance, trade surplus, trade deficit, and trade openness, demonstrating how these measures reflect the health and competitiveness of a country. For instance, Singapore has successfully leveraged trade openness to achieve high-income status and sustained trade-driven growth.

The next chapter explores international trade ideologies and trade theories that have shaped the structure and conduct of cross-border trade among nations. These theoretical perspectives provide a foundational understanding of the rationale behind present-day international trade policies, measures, and regulatory frameworks.

Key Takeaway

1 International trade is a major contributor to a country's GDP, supporting economic growth and development.
2 The trade openness index indicates the extent to which a country is integrated into the global trading system. While most countries maintain a trade openness ratio between 50% and 100%, some countries have exceptionally high trade dependency. For example, Singapore exceeds 300%, underscoring the critical role of international trade in its economy.
3 The balance of trade measures the difference between a country's exports and imports. A trade surplus occurs when exports exceed imports, while a trade deficit occurs when imports exceed exports. However, neither is inherently good or bad; the balance of trade must be assessed in context, alongside GDP, investment, and structural competitiveness.

Notes

1 For further detail, see National Geographic Society (2024, February 10). *The silk road*. https://education.nationalgeographic.org/resource/silk-road/
2 For a detailed discussion on the historical evolution and development of international trade, refer to International Trade Council. (2023). *The evolution of international trade*. https://tradecouncil.org/wp-content/uploads/2024/10/The-Evolution-of-International-Trade.pdf
3 GDP is a crucial tool in economic analysis, but it has its limitations. For example, it does not account for the distribution of income among residents of a country, nor does it measure non-economic factors that contribute to human well-being, like leisure time, environmental quality, and social justice. These limitations have led to the development of alternative measures that aim to provide a more comprehensive picture of economic progress and societal well-being.

Prominent critics including Joseph Stiglitz, a Nobel Laureate in economics, have been vocal critics of GDP as a sole measure of economic success. He advocates for broader measures that consider environmental sustainability and social inclusion. Amartya Sen, another Nobel Laureate, emphasises the need to consider welfare and capabilities rather than just output. He has contributed to developing more comprehensive measures of assessing economic and social progress. However, GDP remains a fundamental indicator of economic activity and a crucial tool in economic planning and policymaking globally. For more detailed discussions, see:

- Stiglitz, J., Sen, A., & Fitoussi, J. (2009). *The measurement of economic performance and social progress*. Retrieved July 21, 2025, from https://ec.europa.eu/eurostat/documents/8131721/8131772/Stiglitz-Sen-Fitoussi-Commission-report.pdf
- Sen, A. (1999). *Development as freedom*. Alfred A. Knopf.
- Sen, A., Fitoussi, J., & Stiglitz, J. (2010). *Mismeasuring our lives: Why GDP doesn't add up*. The New Press.

4 The remaining top ten economies included the United Kingdom (USD 3.38 trillion, growth 0.34%, GDP per capita USD 49,224); France (USD 3.05 trillion, growth 0.94%, GDP per capita USD 45,934); Italy (USD 2.30 trillion, growth 0.7%, GDP per capita USD 38,672); Brazil (USD 2.17 trillion, growth 2.91%); and Canada (USD 2.14 trillion, growth 1.25%, GDP per capita USD 54,517).

An interactive chart on the world GDP can be accessed at: https://data.worldbank.org/indicator/NY.GDP.MKTP.CD?end=2024&most_recent_value_desc=true&skipRedirection=true&start=1960&view=chart

Data sources on GDP by Country are available at Worldometer.(n.d.). https://www.worldometers.info/gdp/gdp-by-country/and the World Bank Group. (n.d.-a). https://data.worldbank.org/indicator/NY.GDP.MKTP.CD?end=2024&start=2024&view=map

5 An interactive chart on countries' trade openness is available at Our World in Data: https://ourworldindata.org/grapher/trade-as-share-of-gdp?tab=chart&country=OWID_WRL~CHN~USA~SGP

6 Data on merchandise trade balance (annual) can be accessed at: https://unctadstat.unctad.org/datacentre/dataviewer/US.TradeMerchBalance

7 The United States has maintained a persistent trade deficit since 1975, marking nearly five decades of continuous net imports of goods. The 1980s marked the beginning of significant trade deficits, largely fuelled by a strong US dollar, increased consumer demand, and the offshoring of manufacturing activities. This pattern intensified in the 1990s and early 2000s with the acceleration of globalisation, the expansion of trade liberalisation agreements, and the rise of China as a dominant exporter. By 2022, the US goods trade deficit had exceeded USD 1.1 trillion, reflecting a structural reliance on imported goods such as electronics, automobiles, apparel, and energy products (Council on Foreign Relations, 2025; Stehrer, 2025).

6

INTERNATIONAL TRADE'S IDEOLOGIES AND THEORETICAL COMPASS

Learning Objectives

1 Understand key international trade theories.
2 Recognise how international trade theories have shaped trade ideologies, policies, and regulatory frameworks.

Specialisation versus Self-Sufficiency: Gains and Limitations

Imagine a situation where one individual excels at preparing main courses while another specialises in desserts. By dividing tasks, both can enjoy a better-quality meal with less effort. This reflects free trade ideology, where countries specialise in producing goods and services in which they hold a comparative advantage, exchanging them internationally for mutual benefit.

Conversely, one might insist on preparing both the main course and dessert alone to become more self-reliant. While this can build skills and protect against dependence, it may lead to inefficiency and inferior outcomes. This mirrors protectionism ideology, where a country limits imports to shield domestic industries, even at the cost of higher prices or lower quality for consumers.

Free trade can enhance efficiency, lower prices, and foster innovation through global competition, but it may also disrupt vulnerable industries, cause job losses, and increase reliance on foreign markets. Protectionism can

DOI: 10.4324/9781003535874-9

safeguard strategic sectors, preserve jobs, and nurture infant industries, yet it often raises costs and limits consumer choice.

In practice, most countries adopt a mixed approach, embracing open trade in certain sectors while applying selective protection measures in areas where economic or social priorities require special attention.

As previous chapters illustrate, international trade plays a critical role in shaping national economies. Over the centuries, a wide array of philosophers, economists, and policy thinkers have offered diverse perspectives on the core questions of international trade: why do countries trade? What should they trade? How do trade patterns form and change? Who gains from trade? And how can nations enhance their competitiveness?

This chapter traces the evolution of international trade thought, from mercantilism and its focus on trade surplus, to classical economic theories that introduced principles such as absolute and comparative advantage, to modern frameworks that account for economies of scale, strategic trade, and competitive advantage. These theoretical contributions have formed international trade ideologies and have significantly influenced international trade policies and regulatory frameworks, shaping how governments and firms navigate the global trading system today.

The formulation of international trade policy is profoundly shaped by ideological perspectives on how economies should engage in cross-border trade. These ideologies shape government decisions on whether to liberalise trade or protect domestic industries, and they often reflect a country's developmental stage and strategic priorities. International trade ideologies can be viewed as existing along a continuum. At one end is protectionism, which emphasises safeguarding domestic industries from foreign competition. Under this approach, exports are actively promoted as a source of national economic strength, while imports are constrained through instruments such as tariffs, quotas, or regulatory barriers to protect local producers, preserve employment, and maintain economic self-sufficiency. At the other end is the ideology of free trade, which calls for minimal government intervention in cross-border exchange. It rests on the premise that unrestricted cross-border exchange allows the most efficient producers to thrive, ultimately promoting global welfare, stimulating innovation, and broadening consumer choice.

Between these two extremes lies a pragmatic middle ground. This approach accepts the benefits of free trade but allows governments to selectively protect or promote industries considered essential to national interests, such as those tied to security, technological leadership, or long-term competitiveness. Each of these ideologies is deeply influenced by international trade theories that have been developed over time, providing the intellectual foundation for policy choices and strategic approaches to global commerce.

Protectionism Ideology: Theoretical Compass

Protectionism ideology is influenced by one of the earliest theories of international trade, dating back to the sixteenth century, so-called mercantilism. It emphasises a nation's accumulation of wealth through a trade surplus, where exports exceed imports. Mercantilists believed that exporting more than importing was the key to national prosperity, and it was in a country's best interest to maintain a trade surplus. According to this view, governments should actively intervene in trade by promoting exports and restricting imports through tariffs and other trade barriers.

A fundamental flaw in this philosophy is the underlying assumption that trade is a zero-sum game, where one country's gain in trade surplus necessarily comes at the expense of another. The theory was criticised by Adam Smith, who advocated for free trade and argued that trade is a positive-sum game. However, certain principles of mercantilism continue to influence modern economic policies that prioritise national interests. For example, protectionism argues that specific industries, particularly emerging or strategic sectors, may need temporary protection from international competition in order to develop the capacity to compete globally. This rationale is commonly referred to as infant industry protection. Protectionist policies are designed to safeguard domestic industries that might otherwise struggle against lower-priced or more efficient foreign goods and services. Such measures are often justified as a way to preserve employment in key sectors, maintain economic stability, and support national development. By restricting imports, governments can help sustain domestic jobs and reduce trade imbalances, particularly when a country faces a persistent trade deficit.

Governments also use protectionism to safeguard public health, safety, and national security. For example, the European Union has banned the import of hormone-treated beef since 1989 due to concerns over potential health risks.[1] Similarly, national security is a common rationale for restricting foreign access to sensitive sectors such as defence, energy, and critical infrastructure. In addition, some governments pursue protectionist policies to achieve greater economic self-sufficiency, reducing reliance on imports of essential goods such as food or critical raw materials in strategic industries.

Free Trade Ideology: Theoretical Compass

The foundations of free trade ideology are deeply rooted in major economic theories, particularly Adam Smith's absolute advantage theory, David Ricardo's Comparative Advantage Theory, and the Heckscher-Ohlin Factor

Endowment Theory. These theories laid the intellectual groundwork for the free trade ideology by emphasising specialisation based on absolute and comparative advantage, efficient allocation of factor endowments (such as labor, capital, and land), and the mutual gains from trade.

Adam Smith's Absolute Advantage Theory

Adam Smith's theory of absolute advantage was first articulated in 'An Inquiry into the Nature and Causes of the Wealth of Nations' (1776). Adam Smith argues that a country should specialise in producing and exporting goods in which it can produce more efficiently than other countries, and import goods in which it is less efficient. By trading these goods, countries can maximise their overall output and economic welfare. International trade is a win-win situation, or a positive-sum game, where both trading partners can achieve mutual gains through increased overall efficiency and resource utilisation and can subsequently improve their economic well-being.

In 'The Wealth of Nations', Adam Smith introduced the concept of absolute advantage with the example of England and Portugal engaging in the trade of cloth and wine. Both countries can produce cloth and wine. However, England can produce cloth more cheaply than Portugal, and Portugal can produce wine more cheaply than England. Therefore, Portugal has an absolute advantage in wine production because it can produce wine at lower cost than England, while England has an absolute advantage in cloth production because it can produce cloth at lower cost than Portugal. Given this, Smith argued that it would be advantageous for Portugal to specialise in the production of wine and for England to specialise in the production of cloth, focusing on their respective efficiencies. They could then trade these goods, benefiting from each other's absolute advantages.

One of Smith's central arguments is the concept of the 'invisible hand'. Through competition and the pursuit of profit, individuals are led to produce goods and services that society demands, resulting in an efficient allocation of resources and the maximisation of wealth for the nation.

David Ricardo's Comparative Advantage Theory

David Ricardo's theory of comparative advantage builds upon Adam Smith's foundational ideas on specialisation and trade. In his seminal work, *Principles of Political Economy and Taxation* (1817), Ricardo introduced the concept that even if a country lacks an absolute advantage in the production of any goods, it can still benefit from international trade by specialising in goods for which it has a comparative advantage, that is, goods it can produce at a lower opportunity cost relative to its trading partners. He argued that mutual gains from trade are possible even when one country is less efficient in producing all goods, as long as each country specialises according to its comparative advantage.

For example, imagine there is a dentist, Dr Alpha, and an assistant, Beta. Dr Alpha is highly skilled in dental care and also capable of performing office administrative tasks, although the latter is not their core expertise. Beta, on the other hand, has no training in dentistry but is competent in administrative work.

Assume Dr Alpha earns $150 per hour performing dental work and could earn $25 per hour doing administrative tasks. Beta, by contrast, generates $20 per hour in administrative work but has zero productivity in dental care. While Dr Alpha is technically capable of doing both tasks, the opportunity cost of performing administrative duties is substantial. Every hour spent on secretarial work represents a loss of $150 in potential dental revenue. Therefore, it is more efficient for Dr Alpha to focus entirely on dentistry and delegate administrative tasks to Beta. For Beta, performing office duties does not involve sacrificing any alternative, making this a mutually beneficial allocation of labour.

This example encapsulates Ricardo's key insight: productivity should be evaluated not in absolute terms, but in terms of what must be given up to produce one good over another. Specialisation according to comparative advantage allows individuals to allocate resources more efficiently and increase overall economic output. Thus, by focusing on their areas of comparative advantage, both Dr Alpha and Beta can maximise the efficiency and productivity of the dental office more effectively than if each tried to do a bit of both tasks. Likewise, by focusing on the production of goods where countries have a comparative advantage, countries can produce these goods at a lower opportunity cost, leading to more efficient global resource utilisation.

David Ricardo's idea supports the notion that free trade leads to an increase in efficiency and welfare for all countries involved, as each country can specialise in producing and exporting goods that use their resources most effectively, while importing goods that would be more costly to produce domestically. This principle has become a cornerstone of free trade policy.

Heckscher–Ohlin's Factor Endowments Theory

The Factor Endowments theory, developed by Eli Heckscher and Bertil Ohlin in the early twentieth century, extends the theory of comparative advantage by identifying factor endowments as its underlying cause. They argued that trade occurs based on differences in factor endowments such as land, labour, natural resources, and capital. Countries would tend to export goods that are intensive in factors of production they have in abundance and import goods that are intensive in factors of production they have in relative scarcity.

For example, the United Arab Emirates, with its rich reserves of oil and natural gas, holds a comparative advantage in energy resources and is a major global exporter of petroleum products. In contrast, Thailand, with its fertile land, favourable climate, and abundant agricultural labour, specialises in exporting agricultural products such as rice, rubber, and tropical fruits. Capital-rich countries like Japan tend to produce and export capital-intensive goods, such as automobiles and precision equipment, while labour-abundant countries such as Bangladesh focus on labour-intensive exports like textiles and garments, which they can produce at lower costs.

Managed/Pragmatic Trade Ideology: Theoretical Compass

Over time, international trade ideologies have been shaped by successive theoretical contributions, from mercantilist doctrine through classical theories to modern frameworks that refine and expand our understanding of trade. For example, Krugman's new trade theory highlights the role of economies of scale and network effects in shaping trade patterns. Similarly, strategic trade policy argues that government intervention can sometimes enhance national welfare by supporting industries with high entry barriers or strong spillover effects, such as aerospace or advanced technologies. Porter's Diamond Theory further emphasises the importance of domestic competitiveness and innovation in driving international success, showing that national advantages arise from dynamic interactions between firms, industries, and government policies. Together, these modern theories offer a more nuanced understanding of why and how governments combine trade openness with targeted strategic interventions to secure sustainable, long-term competitive advantages.

Paul Krugman's New Trade Theory

Paul Krugman's new trade theory (1979, 1980) advances international trade thinking by introducing the importance of economies of scale, network effects, and first-mover advantages into trade theory. Unlike earlier theories of absolute advantage, comparative advantage, and factor endowments, new trade theory highlights how increasing returns to scale, where unit costs fall as production expands, can lead a small number of firms to dominate global markets.[2]

For many products, large-scale production leads to substantial cost efficiencies, known as economies of scale. For instance, manufacturing automobiles in a facility that produces 500,000 units per year is significantly more cost-effective than in one that produces only 5,000 units. These scale advantages encourage countries to specialise in industries where they can achieve scale economies, driving them to seek export markets to absorb higher output levels.

Moreover, the theory underscores the strategic importance of early market entry. Firms that are first movers in an industry can gain long-lasting advantages through learning effects, and network externalities, where the value of a product increases as more people use it (e.g. software, digital platforms). Once established, these advantages can create barriers to entry, making it difficult for latecomers to compete.

Strategic trade policy builds upon and extends the insights of new trade theory. It argues that in industries characterised by oligopolistic competition, high fixed costs, and economies of scale, governments can strategically intervene to enhance national welfare. Such intervention can take several forms. For example, governments may provide subsidies or tax incentives to help domestic firms overcome high entry costs in strategic industries (e.g. aerospace or semiconductors), invest in targeted infrastructure to reduce production or distribution costs, or implement temporary trade measures such as tariffs or quotas to give domestic firms time to build scale and competitiveness. A classic example is the commercial aircraft industry, where government support from European nations enabled Airbus to compete successfully against Boeing, shifting global market share and profits towards Europe. Similarly, the semiconductor industries of South Korea and Taiwan benefited from active state support, allowing them to emerge as global leaders in a sector characterised by substantial economies of scale (Brander & Spencer, 1985).

Porter's Diamond of National Competitive Advantage

Michael Porter's Theory of National Competitive Advantage (1990) offers a comprehensive framework for understanding why certain nations develop globally competitive industries, while others do not – for instance, Japan's global leadership in automobiles or Switzerland's dominance in luxury watches.

Unlike earlier trade theories, Porter's model emphasises the dynamic and systemic nature of competitiveness. He identifies four interrelated determinants that collectively influence a nation's capacity to achieve and sustain competitive advantage in a specific industry:

Factor conditions: This refers to a country's endowment of production factors, both basic (e.g. natural resources) and advanced (e.g. skilled labour, technological capabilities, infrastructure). Porter argues that competitive advantage arises not merely from the abundance of these factors, but from their quality and continuous development. Nations with advanced and specialised resources – such as a well-educated workforce or high-speed logistics infrastructure – are better positioned to produce sophisticated goods and services for global markets.

Demand conditions: Domestic demand plays a crucial role in shaping industry competitiveness. A large, discerning, and sophisticated home market compels firms to innovate, improve product quality, and respond swiftly to evolving customer needs.

Related and supporting industries: The presence of internationally competitive supplier industries and value chain partners enhances a firm's efficiency, innovation, and cost effectiveness. Porter emphasises the importance of industry clusters. A strong network of related and supporting industries can facilitate access to specialised inputs, knowledge sharing, and cost efficiencies, all of which contribute to a country's competitive advantage. For example, a nation with world-class manufacturers of automotive equipment is more likely to develop a robust automotive industry due to the availability of high-quality inputs, faster knowledge transfer, and collaborative innovation.

Firm strategy, structure, and rivalry: This dimension examines how firms are created, organised, and managed, as well as the nature of domestic competition. Nations characterised by intense local rivalry push firms to innovate, upgrade capabilities, and improve productivity. Competitive domestic markets serve as a training ground for firms to develop the resilience and sophistication needed for global competition.

Porter emphasises that the mutual reinforcement of these four factors is key to developing a competitive advantage. When all elements align favourably, they create a self-reinforcing environment that supports innovation, productivity, and international success. Additionally, Porter acknowledges the role of government and chance as influencing variables. Government actions such as subsidies, education policies, infrastructure investment, or regulatory standards can shape any of the four determinants. For instance, subsidies may enhance factor conditions, while rivalry among firms could be influenced by anti-trust laws.[3]

Conclusion

This chapter has traced the evolution of international trade theories, offering insights into why nations engage in trade and how they compete in the global market. These theories form frameworks that help explain the underlying drivers of global trade dynamics. Together, they not only provide a historical and conceptual foundation for understanding trade but also reveal an ideological spectrum ranging from protectionism to free trade. At one extreme, protectionist ideology advocate shielding domestic industries through trade barriers. At the other, free trade ideology champion minimal intervention and open markets. In practice, most nations adopt pragmatic or managed trade approaches, selectively combining protective and liberalising measures based on economic priorities, sectoral sensitivities, and geopolitical considerations. These ideologies continue to shape the formulation of international trade policies and regulatory measures.

Building on this theoretical foundation, the next chapter will explore how these ideologies are translated into real-world trade policies. It will examine the various instruments that governments employ to influence and manage trade flows. These include restrictive measures such as tariffs, quotas, and technical trade barriers, which are often used to protect domestic industries or achieve political goals. The chapter will also analyse a wide range of trade liberalisation mechanisms, such as FTAs and other forms of economic partnerships, which aim to reduce barriers, enhance market access, and promote economic cooperation among nations.

Key Takeaway

1 Protectionism Ideology is rooted in mercantilist principles. It views trade as a zero-sum game, where one nation's gain is another's loss. Nations should aim for a trade surplus to accumulate wealth and strengthen economic power. Strong government control and intervention are essential, using tools such as tariffs, subsidies, quotas, and import restrictions to protect domestic industries.

   Protectionist policy is often justified as a means to preserve jobs, maintain economic stability, protect consumers, and safeguard national security.

2 Free Trade Ideology views trade as a positive-sum game. Countries benefit from trade. It encourages countries to specialise in producing goods in which they are most efficient. Countries export goods they produce efficiently and import goods in which other countries hold an advantage, leading to gains from trade through improved efficiency and specialisation.

3 Trade ideologies exist on a spectrum, with pure protectionism at one end and pure free trade at the other, while most nations adopt pragmatic, mixed approaches that selectively apply both principles depending on sector, geopolitical considerations, and development goals.

   Governments may provide financial support, such as subsidies or tax incentives, to domestic firms to become globally competitive. Tariffs and quotas might be used to shield protected industries from international competition. This protection allows domestic firms to grow large enough to exploit economies of scale without the pressure of competing against established foreign companies. Governments can invest in infrastructure, research and development, and specialised education and training programmes that develop the workforce in a way that aligns with the needs of competitive industries.

Notes

1 For further details, see: European Commission. (n.d.-h). *Hormones in meat*. https://food.ec.europa.eu/food-safety/chemical-safety/hormones-meat_en

2 For further details, see:
- Krugman, P. R. (1979). Increasing returns, monopolistic competition, and international trade. *Journal of International Economics, 9*(4), 469–479.
- Krugman, P. R. (1980). Scale economies, product differentiation, and the pattern of trade. *American Economic Review, 70*(5), 950–959.

3 Many modern indicators have been developed to measure the competitiveness of countries, and competitiveness indices are widely used by policymakers, investors, and business leaders to understand and improve their nations' economic environments. They provide valuable benchmarks that help in comparing performance among countries and in identifying strengths and weaknesses relevant to fostering a competitive economy. For example, the IMD World Competitiveness Ranking, developed by the International Institute for Management Development (IMD) in Switzerland. It analyses how conducive the environment of a country is to achieving sustained business growth. The ranking considers a wide range of factors such as economic performance, government efficiency, business efficiency, and infrastructure. An updated report can be found at IMD. (2025). https://www.imd.org/centers/wcc/world-competitiveness-center/rankings/world-competitiveness-ranking/

The WEF Global Competitiveness is developed by the World Economic Forum. It assesses the competitiveness landscape of economies across the world, offering insight into the drivers of their productivity and prosperity. The WEF defines competitiveness as the set of institutions, policies, and factors that determine the level of productivity of a country. The factors are organised into 12 pillars, which include institutions, infrastructure, macroeconomic stability, health, skills, product market, labour market, financial system, market size, business dynamism, and innovation capability. An updated report can be found at WEF. (2020). https://www.weforum.org/publications/the-global-competitiveness-report-2020/

7

INTERNATIONAL TRADE POLICIES AND MEASURES

Learning Objectives

1. Understand the rationale behind government trade policies and measures, and how they are used to pursue economic and strategic objectives.
2. Learn diverse instruments that governments employ to regulate and facilitate international trade.

How Governments Shape Trade

Trade policies are shaped by a complex interplay of economic, social, strategic, and political considerations. In some cases, governments prioritise economic growth and competitiveness through liberalisation – reducing trade barriers to foster deeper integration. For example, the EU–Singapore FTA, which entered into force in November 2019, eliminated most tariffs and facilitated greater market access, thereby strengthening economic ties and expanding business opportunities for both parties[1].

However, governments also intervene in trade to protect domestic industries, preserve employment, and maintain economic resilience. A notable example is the United States' imposition of tariffs on steel and aluminium in 2018, aimed at shielding domestic producers from low-cost imports and supporting jobs in key sectors.[2]

National security concerns can also strongly influence trade policy. Certain technologies and resources are viewed as too critical to national interests to be

DOI: 10.4324/9781003535874-10

freely transferred abroad. This is evident in the US decision to impose export controls on advanced semiconductor technologies to China, with the goal of safeguarding strategic industries and limiting the proliferation of sensitive technologies.[3]

Moreover, trade can serve as a powerful instrument of foreign policy. Countries may use trade sanctions or embargoes to exert pressure or signal disapproval of another nation's actions. For instance, the European Union imposed sanctions on Russia in response to its invasion of Ukraine.[4]

International trade is a central pillar of the global economy, enabling nations to access a broader range of goods and services, specialise in areas of comparative advantage, and achieve higher levels of economic growth. Yet, the movement of goods and services across borders rarely occurs without government intervention. Driven by economic, political, and social considerations, governments actively shape the terms of trade through a variety of policy instruments, collectively referred to as international trade measures.[5]

On the one hand, international trade measures are used to restrict or regulate trade, shielding domestic industries, preserving employment, protecting consumers, or safeguarding strategic interests such as national security. On the other hand, they aim to promote freer trade, reducing restrictions to enhance economic efficiency, lower consumer prices, attract foreign investment, and strengthen diplomatic and economic ties. Correspondingly, international trade measures can be grouped into two major categories – trade measures to restrict and regulate trade, and trade measures to promote freer trade.

Trade measures to restrict and regulate trade include tariff measures, such as import duties and taxes, and non-tariff measures, such as import quotas, subsidies to domestic industries, and regulatory standards applied to foreign products. They are primarily designed to control the flow of goods across borders, often justified on grounds of protecting domestic producers, maintaining employment levels, ensuring product safety, or protecting sensitive technologies and industries.

In contrast, trade measures to promote free trade or liberalising measures aim to remove or reduce barriers that impede cross-border trade. The most common instruments of trade liberalisation are trade agreements, through which governments negotiate reciprocal commitments to open markets, eliminate tariffs, and streamline regulatory procedures. For example, agreements like the EU–Singapore FTA have eliminated most tariffs while enhancing market access and regulatory cooperation.

It is important to note that, governments' priorities and policy goals are dynamic, varied, and multifaceted. For many countries, a priority and a primary goal is to stimulate economic growth. This leads to the implementation of trade policies designed to create a favourable business environment that encourages investment and enhances competitiveness. For example, governments may reduce tariffs on raw materials to lower import costs, thereby enhancing the competitiveness of the targeted industry.

In certain circumstances, governments may need to prioritise protecting domestic producers, stabilising the local economy, and safeguarding employment. This can involve implementing import–export controls, such as using quotas and tariffs to protect domestic industries or regulating the export of sensitive technologies or materials to specific countries for national security reasons. In addition, political challenges often require managing international relations. In such scenarios, governments might use trade sanctions and embargoes, or retaliatory measures, as diplomatic tools to influence or protest the actions of other nations.

In practice, countries rarely adopt a purely protectionist or fully liberalised approach; rather, they combine restrictive measures with liberalising ones to balance domestic priorities with the benefits of global trade. In the following section, we examine common trade instruments that governments employ. These fall into two broad categories: protectionist measures that restrict imports and shield domestic industries, and trade liberalisation measures that reduce barriers and expand market access.[6]

Protectionist Trade Measures

Tariffs: Tariffs are among the oldest and most straightforward tools governments use to intervene in international trade. A tariff is a tax or duty imposed on imported or exported goods and services. Tariffs can be calculated on two bases: specific tariffs, which are charged as a fixed amount per unit of a good, and ad valorem tariffs, which are calculated as a percentage of the good's value.

Tariffs can be applied to both imports and exports. Import tariffs raise the price of foreign goods, making them less competitive in the domestic market. Export tariffs, on the other hand, can discourage the export of certain goods while also serving as a source of government revenue.

Tariffs benefit governments by generating income and benefit domestic industries by shielding them from foreign competition. By making imported goods more expensive, tariffs can help domestic producers maintain market share. However, these protections come at a cost: consumers face higher prices, and the overall efficiency of the global economy declines. Tariffs may lead to the domestic production of goods that could be produced more efficiently and at a lower cost in other countries.

Quotas: Quotas impose limits on the quantity of specific goods that can be imported or exported during a specific period. Import quotas restrict market access, often leading to higher prices for consumers.

Tariff rate quotas: A tariff rate quota is commonly applied in the agricultural sector. It combines elements of both quotas and tariffs. Under this system, a lower tariff rate is applied to imports up to a specified quota limit, while a higher tariff rate is imposed on quantities exceeding that threshold.

Subsidies: Subsidies are supports provided by governments to domestic producers, aimed at lowering production costs and boosting competitiveness. These supports can take various forms, including direct cash grants, low-interest loans, or tax incentives. Subsidies serve two primary purposes: they help domestic firms compete against lower-cost foreign imports and assist them in expanding into export markets. However, while subsidies can strengthen local industries, they may also shield inefficient producers, encourage overproduction, and shift the financial burden onto consumers who ultimately bear the cost.

Voluntary export restraints (VER): Voluntary export restraints are quotas on trade imposed by the exporting country, usually at the request of the importing country's government. Countries may agree to such arrangements to avoid the risk of facing harsher trade barriers. A notable example is Japan's 1981 decision to voluntarily limit its automobile exports to the United States. By setting its own export limits, Japan sought to prevent the United States from imposing more restrictive and potentially damaging trade measures.[7]

Local content requirements: Local content requirements are a form of trade measure in which governments mandate that a certain percentage of a product be produced domestically. While these requirements support local industries and protect domestic jobs, they often lead to higher production costs and, consequently, increased prices for consumers.

Anti-dumping policies: Dumping refers to the practice of selling goods in a foreign market at prices below their cost of production or below fair market value. This is often done to dispose of surplus goods or, in more aggressive cases, to drive out local competitors through predatory pricing, using profits from home markets to subsidise artificially low prices abroad.

To combat such unfair practices, many countries implement anti-dumping measures by imposing countervailing duties, special tariffs aimed at neutralising the negative effects of dumping on domestic industries.

Administrative policies: Administrative trade policies consist of complex bureaucratic procedures and regulations deliberately designed to hinder or delay imports. Although less visible than tariffs or quotas, these policies can serve as effective non-tariff barriers to trade. Administrative policies take many forms, including:

Customs procedures: Lengthy and complex customs procedures can act as a non-tariff barrier by causing delays and adding costs to trade. Some countries impose quality and inspection requirements, including rigorous inspection and certification requirements on imported goods, which can increase costs and delay shipments.

Export/import licenses and permits: Governments may require export/import licenses or permits for certain goods. This adds administrative burdens and can be used to limit exports and imports.

Standards and technical requirements: These may include product quality standards, manufacturing standards, safety standards, and sanitary and phytosanitary measures. While such standards are often essential to ensure safety and quality, they can become trade barriers when applied in an excessive, arbitrary, or discriminatory manner.

Embargoes: They constitute a special category of restrictive measures, often motivated by political, ethical, or security concerns rather than purely economic reasons. An embargo is a government-imposed ban or severe restriction on trade with a specific country or on specific products (e.g. arms embargoes). Such measures are typically used to pressure governments to change certain behaviours, comply with international law, or protect national security.

Trade Liberalisation Measures

Trade liberalisation measures are rooted in free trade ideology, which advocates for the international exchange of goods and services with minimal government restrictions or barriers. These policies aim to stimulate economic growth by expanding markets and encouraging investment. Increased trade often leads to job creation and income growth, whilst consumers benefit from access to a wider variety of goods and services at competitive prices.

One of the key international trade policies to promote trade liberalisation is through 'Regional economic integration'. Regional economic integration refers to agreements among countries within a specific geographic area to reduce or eliminate tariff and non-tariff barriers, promoting the free movement of goods, services, and factors of production across borders. A prime example of a country with a high level of trade openness is Singapore. Singapore is particularly active in pursuing trade agreements as part of its economic strategy, owing to its small size and limited natural resources, making it heavily dependent on trade. Singapore's FTAs encompass a wide array of partnerships both regionally and globally, including bilateral FTAs with the United States, China, Japan, Korea, and India, as well as agreements with the European Union, the European Free Trade Association (EFTA), and the Comprehensive and Progressive Agreement for Trans-Pacific Partnership (CPTPP). Over the years, it has established a broad network of 27 implemented trade agreements. These agreements significantly enhance Singapore's access to global markets, making it one of the most open and trade-friendly economies in the world.[8]

Theoretically, there are five levels of regional economic integration.[9] Each level represents a further step towards economic integration, typically requiring greater commitments and reductions in national sovereignty as member countries coordinate more closely.

Free trade area: Countries in a free trade area agree to eliminate trade barriers within the area but maintain their own external trade policies.

Customs union: This goes a step further by not only allowing free trade among member countries but also adopting a common external trade policy against non-members. This means all members charge the same tariffs on goods coming from outside the union.

Common market: A common market represents a deeper form of economic integration beyond a customs union. In a common market, member countries not only remove barriers to trade, but also allow the free movement of labour and capital across borders.

Economic union: This involves the integration of economic policies, extending beyond a common market to encompass unified fiscal and monetary policies among member countries.

Political union (or complete economic integration): This is the deepest form of economic integration. It entails a complete political and economic integration where member countries unify their economic and political policies and governing institutions.

The following examples demonstrate various forms of regional economic integration worldwide.

Examples of Regional Economic Integration in Americas

North American Free Trade Agreement (NAFTA): Signed in 1994 among the United States, Canada, and Mexico, NAFTA aimed to eliminate trade barriers and increase investment among the three countries. This landmark trade agreement remained in effect until it was replaced by the *United States–Mexico–Canada Agreement (USMCA)* in 2020. The USMCA updated and modernised several aspects of NAFTA to address contemporary trade issues, including significant changes in automotive rules of origin, strengthened labour provisions, adjustments to intellectual property rights, and provisions for the digital economy.[10]

Mercosur, officially known as the Southern Common Market, is a South American trade bloc established in 1991 by the Treaty of Asunción, with Argentina, Brazil, Paraguay, and Uruguay as its founding members. The bloc was created with the primary aim of promoting free trade, regional economic integration, and the free movement of goods, services, capital, and people across member countries. Venezuela was later admitted as a full member in

2012 but has been suspended since December 2016 due to concerns related to democratic governance and human rights (MERCOSUR, n.d.). Mercosur has actively pursued external trade agreements, most notably with the European Union, with whom it reached the agreement in 2024 following more than two decades of negotiations (European Commission, n.d.-g; AP, 2024). The bloc continues to serve as a central platform for economic cooperation in Latin America and plays an influential role in shaping regional trade policy.[11]

The Andean Community (Comunidad Andina, CAN): This is a customs union composed of Bolivia, Colombia, Ecuador, and Peru, established through the foundational Cartagena Agreement signed on May 26, 1969. The bloc aims to deepen economic integration by establishing a customs union and a common external tariff to facilitate the expansion of regional markets and to foster sustainable development while striving to maintain high employment levels (Comunidad Andina, n.d.-a). The Andean Community's institutional framework, comprising bodies such as the Andean Presidential Council, the Commission, and the Secretariat General, supports coordinated policymaking and institutional governance across member states (Comunidad Andina, n.d.-c). This integration extends to external economic ties, notably through the EU–CAN trade agreement, which has been in provisional application since 2013 and expanded in subsequent years (European Commission, n.d.-c).[12]

The Caribbean Community (CARICOM): This was established on July 4, 1973, by the signing of the Treaty of Chaguaramas, with the primary objectives of advancing economic integration, promoting cooperation among member states, and ensuring that the benefits of integration are shared equitably across the region. CARICOM also coordinates foreign policy positions among its members and implements joint strategies in international forums to strengthen the collective voice of Caribbean nations (CARICOM, n.d.-a, n.d.-b).[13]

Examples of Regional Economic Integration in Europe

In Europe, regional economic integration is highly advanced, featuring several key initiatives that promote economic cooperation, reduce trade barriers, and foster collective economic growth.

The European Union (EU) is widely recognised as the most developed and comprehensive model of regional economic integration in the world. It consists of 27 member states united under a legal and institutional framework aimed at promoting economic, political, and social cooperation (European Commission, n.d.-a). One of the European Union's core achievements is the establishment of a single market, which guarantees the free movement of goods, services, capital, and persons across its territory, supported by harmonised laws and regulatory alignment (European Commission, n.d.-b).

The Union also administers a common trade policy, enabling it to engage in trade negotiations as a unified bloc (European Commission, n.d.-a).

Moreover, the European Union has developed a monetary union known as the Eurozone, formed on January 1, 1999. This monetary integration includes 20 of the 27 EU member states, all of which have adopted the euro as their official currency (European Commission, n.d.-c, n.d.-l, n.d.-m; European Central Bank, n.d.). The adoption of a common currency has reduced transaction costs, stabilised exchange rates, and enhanced economic integration, supporting deeper intra-European trade and investment.[14]

The European Free Trade Association (EFTA) was founded on January 4, 1960, through the EFTA Convention. It comprises four member states, namely Iceland, Liechtenstein, Norway, and Switzerland, and aims to promote free trade through an extensive global network of FTAs (European Free Trade Association, n.d.-a, n.d.-b, n.d.-c).[15]

Examples of Regional Economic Integration in Africa

African Continental Free Trade Area (AfCFTA): AfCFTA was officially established on March 21, 2018, in Kigali, Rwanda, where 44 African Union (AU) member states signed the agreement, and trading commenced on January 1, 2021. As of 2023, the AU has 54 member states participating in the agreement, making it the largest free trade area in the world by number of participating countries (World Economic Forum, 2023).

AfCFTA aims to create a single market for goods and services across Africa. According to the World Economic Forum (2023), AfCFTA connects 1.3 billion people across 54 countries with a combined GDP of USD 3.4 trillion. The World Bank (2020) highlighted that the potential benefits of AfCFTA could be transformative, as it could lift 30 million people out of extreme poverty and raise Africa's real income by USD 450 billion by 2035. Nonetheless, significant challenges remain. These include infrastructure deficits, non-tariff barriers, weak institutional capacity, regulatory misalignments, and regional disparities (World Bank, 2020).

East African Community (EAC): EAC comprises seven member states: Burundi, the Democratic Republic of the Congo, Kenya, Rwanda, South Sudan, Tanzania, and Uganda. Initially founded in 1967, the EAC collapsed in 1977 but was re-established in 2000. Headquartered in Arusha, Tanzania, the EAC aims to broaden and deepen cooperation among partner states across economic, social, and political spheres. Its objectives include advancing regional integration, accelerating sustainable development, and achieving shared prosperity (EAC Secretariat, 2023).

Economic Community of West African States (ECOWAS): ECOWAS is a regional bloc of 15 West African countries, established in 1975 through the

Treaty of Lagos. Its current members are: Benin, Burkina Faso, Cape Verde, Côte d'Ivoire, Gambia, Ghana, Guinea, Guinea-Bissau, Liberia, Mali, Niger, Nigeria, Senegal, Sierra Leone, and Togo. Its headquarters is in Abuja, Nigeria. ECOWAS aims to promote economic integration across multiple sectors, including industry, trade, agriculture, transport, telecommunications, energy, and monetary and financial policies. It also plays a key role in political cooperation, especially in conflict resolution, democratic transitions, and peacekeeping operations (African Union, n.d.-b).

However, the EAC and ECOWAS face key challenges, including non-tariff barriers and customs inefficiencies, uneven economic development and disparities among member states, political tensions and security concerns. Still, they remain one of the most structured and ambitious regional blocs in Africa (African Union, n.d.-a, n.d.-b, n.d.-c; Office of the United States Trade Representative, n.d.-b).

Examples of Regional Economic Integration in Asia

Association of Southeast Asian Nations (ASEAN): ASEAN was established on August 8, 1967. It comprises eleven member states: Brunei, Cambodia, Indonesia, Laos, Malaysia, Myanmar, the Philippines, Singapore, Thailand, Timor-Leste,[16] and Vietnam. The organisation aims to foster political and economic cooperation, enhance regional integration, and promote stability across Southeast Asia.

ASEAN Free Trade Area (AFTA): AFTA was established in 1992 with the aim of creating a free trade area to increase ASEAN's competitive edge as a production base in the global market. AFTA aimed to reduce tariffs and non-tariff barriers among ASEAN countries, facilitating freer movement of goods within the region. ASEAN is progressing towards a more comprehensive economic integration through the ASEAN Economic Community (AEC). This included not just trade in goods, but also services, investment, skilled labour, and capital, building a more integrated and cohesive economy, enhanced connectivity, and a resilient, inclusive ASEAN. Besides promoting a more integrated economy within ASEAN, the organisation has established several trade agreements with external partners to expand regional market access and economic cooperation. Examples are ASEAN–China Free Trade Area (ACFTA), ASEAN–Korea Free Trade Area (AKFTA), ASEAN–Japan Comprehensive Economic Partnership (AJCEP), ASEAN–Australia–New Zealand FTA (AANZFTA), ASEAN–India Free Trade Area (AIFTA) (ASEAN, n.d.-a, n.d.-b).

Asia-Pacific Economic Cooperation (APEC): Established in 1989, APEC comprises 21 Pacific Rim economies and serves as a regional forum promoting free trade, economic cooperation, and sustainable growth throughout the Asia-Pacific region. Member countries are Australia, Brunei Darussalam,

Canada, Chile, People's Republic of China, Hong Kong, China, Indonesia, Japan, Republic of Korea (South Korea), Malaysia, Mexico, New Zealand, Papua New Guinea, Peru, Philippines, Russia, Singapore, Chinese Taipei (Taiwan), Thailand, United States, and Vietnam. Together, these economies represent over 2.9 billion people (about 38% of the world's population), approximately 62% of the global GDP, and nearly 48% of global trade (APEC, 2024).

The Comprehensive and Progressive Agreement for Trans-Pacific Partnership (CPTPP): This landmark trade agreement among 11 Asia-Pacific countries evolved from the Trans-Pacific Partnership (TPP) after the United States withdrew in 2017. The original TPP was signed on February 4, 2016, in Auckland, New Zealand, and aimed to deepen economic ties between member countries, reduce tariffs, and foster trade and investment among member countries.

Following the US withdrawal in January 2017, the remaining 11 countries proceeded with a modified agreement, transforming the TPP into the CPTPP. The CPTPP was signed on March 8, 2018, in Santiago, Chile, and includes Australia, Brunei, Canada, Chile, Japan, Malaysia, Mexico, New Zealand, Peru, Singapore, and Vietnam. The CPTPP represents one of the world's largest free trade areas, covering approximately 13.4% of the global economy.[17]

Regional Comprehensive Economic Partnership (RCEP): Signed on November 15, 2020, RCEP is a comprehensive agreement among the ASEAN member states plus China, Japan, South Korea, Australia, and New Zealand. As the world's largest trading bloc by population and economic output, it encompasses more than two billion people and accounts for approximately 30% of global GDP. RCEP aims to reduce tariffs, establish common rules of origin, and facilitate trade and investment flows across the Asia-Pacific region (World Economic Forum, 2021; APEC, 2022).

It is worth noting that modern regional economic integration can extend beyond traditional geographic proximity to include key trading partners, even if they are not contiguous. This trend reflects the shift towards globalisation and the strategic economic interests that drive nations to form alliances based on mutual benefits rather than just proximity. This is because modern trade is increasingly characterised by complex supply chains, where production processes are spread across multiple countries. Countries seek to integrate economically with key partners that play significant roles in their global supply chains, regardless of geographic location. This form of integration helps in optimising supply chains and reducing costs. For instance, a study by the World Trade Organization (2023a) titled 'Global Value Chain Development Report' highlights how GVCs drive economic policies and integration efforts, focusing on strategic economic partners rather than mere geographic neighbours. Nations often enter into trade agreements with countries that offer strategic economic advantages, such as technology partnerships, access to critical raw materials, or large markets. For example, the CPTPP and RCEP include countries from multiple continents, indicating a shift towards forming alliances based on shared economic interests and strategic benefits rather than geographic closeness.

What Are the Right Policies? Free Trade or Protectionism?

Several contemporary works continue to explore the complexities and challenges of international trade policies in a modern, interconnected world. For example, Wolf (2004) and Bhagwati (2004) provide a strong defence of free trade, arguing how it has led to prosperity and reduced poverty worldwide. Similarly, Friedman's (2005) *The World is Flat: A Brief History of the Twenty First Century* discusses how globalised trade has flattened the world, arguing that globalisation levels the competitive playing fields between industrial and emerging market countries.

Although free trade brings many benefits, it also faces criticisms and challenges. For example, Polanyi (1944) argued against the idea that free trade is inherently beneficial for all parties involved. He believed that unregulated markets and unchecked free trade could trigger social disruption and economic instability. In a contemporary work, Stiglitz (2002) – a Nobel Prize-winning economist – has voiced his criticisms of certain aspects of free trade, particularly concerning vulnerable economies and issues of inequality and social justice. He argues that trade liberalisation and globalisation have frequently failed to deliver their anticipated benefits. Rather than fostering stability and equitable growth, they have often exacerbated economic volatility, deepened income inequality, and heightened social insecurity. The underlying assumption that market liberalisation inherently leads to efficient resource allocation and sustained economic growth has proven to be overly simplistic. In many instances, the adverse consequences of globalisation have disproportionately impacted the poorest segments of society.

Dani Rodrik, in *The Globalisation Paradox: Democracy and the Future of the World Economy* (2011), argues that the push towards hyper-globalisation, characterised by extensive economic integration and global economic rules, comes at the expense of national sovereignty. He contends that this tension creates significant challenges for democratic governance. Rodrik suggests that instead of pursuing an absolute form of global economic integration, a more moderate approach to globalisation is beneficial. This approach respects national borders and allows governments to adopt policies that best suit their economic circumstances and priorities. Rodrik highlights that different nations require different solutions and that policies effective in one country may not be suitable for another. This diversity necessitates flexibility in global economic rules to accommodate various national strategies for development and social welfare. Rodrik advocates for a rebalanced form of globalisation that not only promotes open markets but also permits countries the space to set their own policies on capital flows, investments, and trade to suit their unique developmental and social objectives.

Given that both protectionism and free trade offer distinct advantages as well as inherent drawbacks, governments often find it pragmatic to employ a combination of both strategies. While free trade can stimulate economic efficiency, innovation, and consumer access to a broader range of goods, it may also expose vulnerable industries to heightened competition and job loss in certain industries. Conversely, protectionist measures can safeguard domestic employment and strategic sectors but may also result in inefficiencies, higher consumer prices, and retaliatory trade actions. In response to these trade-offs, governments are likely to implement a hybrid approach, mixing trade policies that include elements of both free trade and protectionism. This blended approach allows countries to balance the economic benefits of open markets with the need to protect domestic industries and maintain economic stability. The balance between free trade and protectionism can shift based on a country's economic and social priorities, political climate, and external economic conditions. For example, during periods of economic growth, a country might lean towards more free trade policies to maximise the benefits from international markets. In times of economic stress or when key industries are threatened by foreign competition, a country might impose or increase protectionist measures to shield domestic businesses and jobs.

Conclusion

This chapter has highlighted why and how governments strategically manage trade flows through a wide range of international trade measures. Protectionist trade measures, such as tariffs, quotas, subsidies, and regulatory standards, are implemented to protect domestic industries, preserve employment, ensure consumer safety, and safeguard strategic interests. In contrast, trade liberalisation measures aim to promote free trade by reducing barriers and fostering deeper integration through bilateral, regional, or multilateral trade agreements.

In practice, no country pursues a purely protectionist or fully liberalised international trade policies. Instead, governments carefully balance these two approaches to meet economic, political, and social objectives. The next part of this book, Why International Trade Laws and Regulations Matter, bridges the business and economic dimensions of trade with the legal frameworks and their practical application in international commerce. It will examine the legal foundation governing global trade, including Key Principles of Incoterms®, Customs Formalities Processes, and Key Contracts in International Trade.

Key Takeaway

1. International trade measures fall into two broad categories. Those that restrict or regulate trade (protectionist trade measures) and those that promote free trade (trade liberalisation measures).
2. Protectionist tools such as tariffs, quotas, and subsidies are used to protect domestic industries from foreign competition, safeguard employment, and correct trade imbalances.
3. Free trade policies, by reducing or eliminating trade barriers, encourage competition, drive efficiency and innovation, and offer consumers greater choice at lower prices. They also enable countries to specialise in industries where they hold a comparative advantage.
4. Countries rarely rely solely on protectionism or pure liberalisation; instead, they combine both approaches to balance domestic priorities with global competitiveness. This balance can shift based on economic and social conditions, political changes, and international relations. In situations where domestic industries are vulnerable, trade barriers provide a buffer against foreign competition. Conversely, in industries where a country holds a comparative advantage, free trade policies help expand markets and drive growth. The key is to strike a balance that maximises national benefits while fostering global trade relations.

Notes

1 For further details, see European Commission. (2019, November 21).

2 For further details, see Sachdev, V., & Rao, A. (2025, March 11).

3 For further details, see US Department of Commerce, Bureau of Industry and Security. (2024, December 2), and Triolo, P. (n.d.).

4 For further details, see European Commission. (n.d.-j), and Norman, L., & Pancevski, B. (2025, July 18).

5 In international economics, the term 'trade barriers' is commonly used to describe policies that restrict the flow of goods and services across borders. These barriers are typically classified into two types: *tariff barriers (TB)*, such as taxes, import duties, and *non-tariff barriers (NTBs)*. NTBs encompass a wide range of restrictions and regulations that affect international trade without involving direct taxes or duties. NTBs can take various forms, for example, quotas, subsidies, and regulatory standards.

By contrast, the term *trade measures* is broader in nature, encompassing not only restrictive policies but also those designed to liberalise and facilitate trade.

6 For a more detailed explanation on trade measures and the various tools governments commonly adopt to regulate cross-border commerce, see Hill, C. W. L. (2023). *International business: Competing in the global marketplace*. McGraw-Hill Education.

7 For further details, see Cohen, S. (n.d.). *The route to Japan's voluntary export restraints on automobiles*. https://nsarchive2.gwu.edu/japan/scohenwp.htm

8 Details of Singapore's FTAs can be found at the Ministry of Trade and Industry, https://www.mti.gov.sg/Trade/Free-Trade-Agreements

9 Bela Balassa formulated the theory of economic integration levels in his book *The Theory of Economic Integration* (1961), which outlines several stages of integration, including free trade area, customs union, common market, economic union, and complete economic integration, providing a clear framework for understanding the different depths of integration agreements. For a broader discussion of regional economic integration concepts in international business, see Hill (2023).

10 For detailed information on the transition from NAFTA to USMCA, see Office of the United States Trade Representative. (n.d.-c). *United States–Mexico–Canada agreement.* https://ustr.gov/trade-agreements/free-trade-agreements/united-states-mexico-canada-agreement

11 For further details, see the official MERCOSUR website: https://www.mercosur.int/en

12 For further details, see Comunidad Andina's website: http://www.comunidadandina.org/

13 For further information, see the official CARICOM website: https://caricom.org/

14 For more information on EU membership, its single market, and Eurozone entry criteria, see the official EU portal: https://european-union.europa.eu/

15 Further details can be found on the official EFTA website: https://www.efta.int/

16 Timor-Leste was formally admitted as the newest member state of ASEAN at the 47th ASEAN Summit in Kuala Lumpur, Malaysia, on October 26, 2025.

17 While there is no single centralised official website for the Comprehensive and Progressive Agreement for Trans-Pacific Partnership (CPTPP), authoritative information is available through official government sources from member economies. Key sources include:

- The New Zealand Ministry of Foreign Affairs and Trade. https://www.mfat.govt.nz/en/trade/free-trade-agreements/free-trade-agreements-in-force/cptpp/
- Government of Canada. https://www.international.gc.ca/trade-commerce/trade-agreements-accords-commerciaux/agr-acc/cptpp-ptpgp/index.aspx
- Ministry of Trade and Industry Singapore (MTI). https://www.mti.gov.sg/Trade/Free-Trade-Agreements/CPTPP

PART 4

Why Do International Trade Laws and Regulations Matter?

8

KEY PRINCIPLES OF INTERNATIONAL COMMERCIAL TERMS (INCOTERMS®)

Learning Objectives

1 Understand the significance of Incoterms in international trade.
2 Recognise costs and risks associated with each international trade term.
3 Determine the appropriate Incoterms based on obligations and risk levels in different trade scenarios.

Why Does Clarity of Trade Terms Matter?

Imagine this scenario: A Chinese seller exports glassware to the United Kingdom for £5,000. The UK buyer assumes this price covers all expenses, including transportation and customs clearance. They expect to pay £5,000 with no extra charges upon receiving the goods.

However, the Chinese seller only commits to delivering the products to the buyer's premises, not covering import customs clearance, duties, and taxes. When the goods arrive, the UK buyer refuses them, insisting the seller should handle import customs clearance and taxes.

International trade pricing can be complicated and differ significantly from domestic transactions. Exporters must carefully consider their obligations and risks for which they are responsible. To provide an accurate price quotation, exporters and importers must clearly define the terms and conditions of sale. For example, who is responsible for pre-carriage[1], main-carriage[2], and on-carriage[3]? Who manages the export customs formalities process? Who

DOI: 10.4324/9781003535874-12

is responsible for import duties and taxes? If a product is damaged during transportation, who bears responsibility for the damage? Undefined responsibilities regarding costs and risks can lead to misunderstandings, delays, extra expenses, trade disputes, and potential damage to the business relationship.

In international trade, we use Incoterms[4] to help identify responsibilities for costs relevant to delivering the goods to the customer and transfer points of risk from the seller to the buyer. They provide a common, internationally recognised language that clearly and precisely defines delivery, costs, and risk allocation, hence avoiding confusion and misunderstandings when incorporated into contracts of sale. International trade can become costly if one does not understand the rules of the Incoterms.

What Are Incoterms®?

The Incoterms® have been developed by the International Chamber of Commerce (ICC), based in Paris, France.[5] The primary aim is to establish a common set of rules and guidelines that facilitate international trade and reduce misunderstandings among traders of different countries. Each Incoterms rule defines the responsibilities of the buyer and the seller regarding the delivery of goods, the transfer of risks, and the division of costs.[6]

Incoterms were first published in 1936. Over the years, Incoterms have been revised multiple times to accommodate the evolving complexities of international trade and ensure that the terms remain relevant and effective. The revisions have aimed to address issues such as the rise of new transportation methods, advancements in technology, and the increasing globalisation of trade. Significant revisions include those made in 1953, 1967, 1976, 1980, 1990, 2000, 2010, and the most recent revision in 2020.[7]

Incoterms 2020 comprises 11 terms, categorised into two groups.

The first group is Incoterms for Any Mode or Modes of Transport. There are seven terms, namely Ex Works (EXW); Free Carrier (FCA); Carriage Paid To (CPT); Carriage and Insurance Paid To (CIP); Delivered at Place (DAP); Delivered at Place Unloaded (DPU); and Delivered Duty Paid (DDP).

The second group is Incoterms for Sea and Inland Waterway Transport. This group comprises of four terms, namely Free Alongside Ship (FAS); Free on Board (FOB); Cost and Freight (CFR); and Cost, Insurance, and Freight (CIF).

Structurally, ICC provides a set of rules of interpretation for the obligations of both the seller (A1–A10) and the buyer (B1–B10) covering ten key issues, which have been depicted in Figure 8.3.

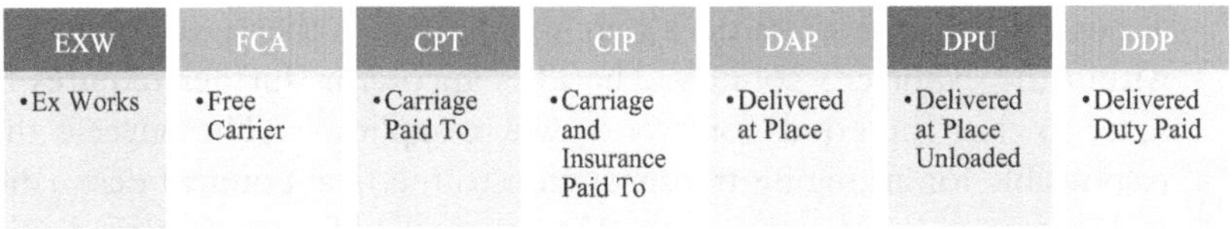

FIGURE 8.1 Incoterms for any modes of transport.

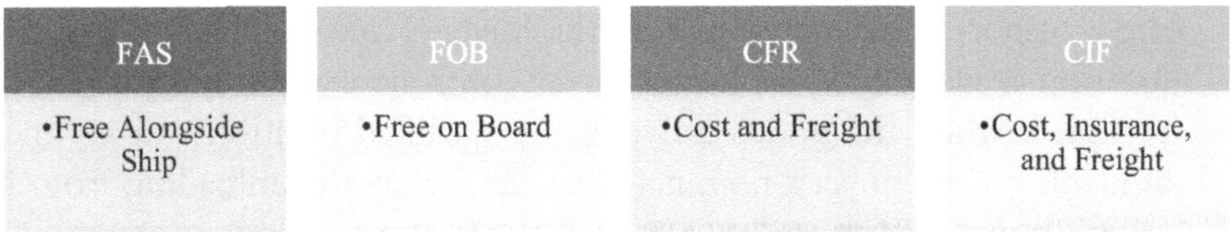

FIGURE 8.2 Incoterms for sea and inland waterway transport.

FIGURE 8.3 Obligations under ICC Incoterms for sellers and buyers.

Terms and Definitions of Incoterms 2020[8]

1. **Ex Works (EXW) (insert named place of delivery)**
   This term is applicable to all modes of transport. Under EXW, the seller bears minimal responsibility, limited to making the goods available for pickup at their warehouse, factory, or another agreed location on the specified date. The buyer is responsible for loading the goods at the seller's premises and assumes all subsequent costs and risks, covering transportation, handling, and related procedures from the point of pickup to final delivery. The buyer is also fully responsible for both export and import clearance, including all associated duties and documentation.

   The seller bears all risks of loss or damage to the goods until they are handed over to the buyer at the agreed-upon premises on the agreed-upon date specified in the sales contract.
2. **Free Carrier (FCA) (insert named place of delivery)**
   Under FCA, the seller is responsible for delivering the goods at their own expense to a specified location. This location can be a seaport, rail terminal,

airport, the freight forwarder's warehouse, or any other agreed-upon site within the exporter's country. The FCA Incoterms further requires the seller to clear the goods for export, where applicable. The buyer is then responsible for arranging transportation to the final point of destination and import clearance procedures. No insurance obligation is placed either on the seller or on the buyer.

Regarding the delivery point, if the designated place of delivery is the seller's premises, delivery is complete once the goods are loaded onto the transport vehicle arranged by the buyer. However, if the designated location is elsewhere, such as a buyer-controlled warehouse, delivery is complete when the goods arrive at the specified location and are made available to the buyer's nominated carrier, ready for unloading from the seller's transport vehicle.[9]

3. **Free Alongside Ship (FAS) (insert named port of loading)**
This term applies to the sea and inland waterway modes of transport. According to the FAS Incoterms, the seller is responsible for all the costs prior to placing the goods alongside the vessel at the port of shipment within reach of its loading equipment so that they can be loaded aboard the ship. The seller has an obligation to clear the goods for export. The buyer bears all expenses regarding the carriage of the goods from the named port of shipment to its destination, and loading the goods onto the vessel. The import clearance procedures and duties are the responsibility of the buyer.
The risk of loss or damage to the goods transfers from the seller to the buyer once the goods are placed alongside the vessel designated by the buyer at the specified port of shipment.
4 **Free on Board (FOB) (insert named port of loading)**
The FOB term applies exclusively to sea and inland waterway modes of transport. It is similar to FAS, with the key difference being that under FOB, the seller is also responsible for loading the goods onto the vessel in due time, bearing all associated costs and risks up to that point. The seller is also responsible for export clearance. From the moment the goods are loaded on board at the named port of shipment, all transportation costs, import procedures, and duties are borne by the buyer.
The risk of product loss or damage is transferred from the seller to the buyer when the goods are placed on board the vessel nominated by the buyer at the named port of shipment.
5. **Cost and Freight (CFR) (insert named port of destination)**
The term CFR applies to the sea and inland waterway modes of transport. Under CFR, the seller has to arrange and pay for the shipment of goods to the port of destination. The export customs formalities are also the seller's responsibility. The buyer is obliged to pay all the costs after the arrival of the vessel at the destination. Therefore, the buyer is responsible for the costs of unloading the goods at the port of destination and all the

local charges at destination, import duties and taxes, as well as any additional transportation costs to the final destination.

The risk is transferred from the seller to the buyer once the cargo is loaded on board the ship at the loading port.

6. **Cost, Insurance, and Freight (CIF) (insert named port of destination)**

   This term applies to the sea and inland waterway modes of transport. Under CIF, the seller's obligations are the same as under CFR, with the added responsibility of obtaining cargo insurance under Clauses (C) of the Institute Cargo Clauses.[10] This insurance must cover the buyer's risk of loss or damage to the goods during transit, from the point of delivery up to at least the port of destination, for a value of 110% of the contract price in the agreed currency. The seller must also provide the buyer with proof of insurance. The buyer is responsible for the costs of unloading the goods at the destination port, import duties and taxes, as well as any additional transport costs to the final destination.

   The risk passes to the buyer when the cargo is loaded on the vessel at the loading port.

7. **Carriage Paid To (CPT) (insert named place of destination)**

   The CPT term applies to all modes of transport. Under this term, the seller is responsible for export clearance and must arrange and pay for the transportation of goods to the agreed destination in the importing country. The buyer is responsible for import customs procedures and any additional transport beyond the named destination.

   The risk of loss or damage transfers from the seller to the buyer once the goods are handed over to the first carrier in the exporting country. It is important to note that under CPT, the seller's cost responsibility continues up to the named place of destination, as they must pay for transport to that point. However, the risk transfers much earlier (once the goods are handed over to the first carrier at the place of shipment). This distinction means that the seller bears the cost of delivery beyond the point at which they no longer bear the risk of loss or damage.

8. **Carriage and Insurance Paid to (CIP) (insert named place of destination)**

   The CIP term applies to any mode of transport. Under the CIP Incoterms, the seller has the same obligations as under the CPT Incoterms, with the additional obligation to arrange cargo insurance. The minimum level of insurance coverage is 110% of the contractual price, and it shall be made in conformity with Clauses (A) of the Institute Cargo Clauses. Once contracted, the seller has an obligation to provide the insurance policy to the buyer.

   The seller's risk ends when the goods are handed over to the first carrier.

9. **Delivered at Place (DAP) (insert named place of destination)**

   The DAP term applies to any mode of transport. Under DAP, the seller is responsible for delivering goods to an agreed location in the buyer's country, placing the goods at the buyer's disposal, not unloaded. The exporter is responsible for the export clearance. The buyer is responsible for unloading cargo at the destination and clearing goods for import.

Risk is transferred to the buyer once the goods reach at the named place of destination, ready for unloading by the buyer.

10. **Delivered at Place Unloaded (DPU) (insert named place of destination)**[11]
The DPU term applies to any mode of transport. Under DPU, the seller is responsible for delivering goods to the buyer at a named terminal, port, or place of destination in the buyer's country, unloading them from the transport vehicle, and placing the goods at the buyer's disposal. The exporter is responsible for export clearance. The buyer handles the import clearance procedures and transports goods further if necessary.
The risk is transferred from the seller to the buyer once the goods are unloaded from the vehicle and placed at the disposal of the buyer at the destination. Note that among the Incoterms, it is only the DPU that requires the seller to unload goods at the destination.
11. **Delivered Duty Paid (DDP) (named place of destination)**
This term is applicable to all modes of transport. Under DDP, the seller bears full responsibility for delivering the goods to the named place in the country of import, covering all costs and risks involved, including import customs clearance and payment of duties and taxes. The buyer's sole obligation is to unload the goods upon delivery.
DDP places the greatest level of responsibility on the seller and is the only Incoterm that requires the seller to handle import clearance.

Cautions in Using Incoterms

Always incorporate the Incoterms rules into the sales contract. Incoterms help identify responsibilities for costs relevant to delivering goods to customers and determine when risk transfers from the exporter to the importer. They establish a shared language that clearly defines delivery obligations and risk allocation, mitigating confusion and misunderstandings.

However, Incoterms rules are neither laws nor a substitute for a sales contract. Instead, they serve as a standardised framework that outlines the responsibilities, obligations, risk and cost allocations between the seller and the buyer in international transactions. On one hand, they define the point of delivery, indicating when the risk of loss or damage to the goods transfers from the seller to the buyer. On the other hand, they clarify which party is responsible for specific costs, including transportation, insurance, documentation, and customs formalities.

By providing a common language and eliminating ambiguity across jurisdictions, Incoterms have significantly simplified international trade negotiations. Nonetheless, they do not cover every aspect of a sales contract. For instance, Incoterms do not address:

- Specifications of the goods.
- Transfer of legal ownership (title) of the goods from the seller to the buyer.
- Payment method, payment terms, currency, and payment timing.
- Required customs documentation for customs clearance.
- Liability in cases of non-conformity with the sales contract.
- The consequences of a breach of contract.
- Dispute resolution methods and governing law.

It is crucial to understand that although Incoterms provide a vital framework within the sales agreement, they cannot replace it. The sales contract stands as the sole comprehensive document, embodying all the terms and conditions mutually agreed upon by the seller and the buyer.

Always specify the version of Incoterms. Given the multitude of Incoterms versions, it is advisable to always specify the version of Incoterms being used to prevent miscommunication by adding the respective year.

Clearly identify the designated place or port. It is essential to precisely designate the place or port to avoid confusion regarding delivery points and costs. For instance, 'FCA BFS Cargo, Suvarnabhumi Airport, Thailand, Incoterms 2020' offers greater precision and clarity compared to simply stating 'FCA Suvarnabhumi Airport'.

Select the appropriate Incoterms rule. For instance, Incoterms FAS, FOB, CFR, and CIF are exclusively intended for marine and waterway transport, while EXW, FCA, CPT, CIP, DAP, DPU, and DDP are suitable for any mode of transport.

Consideration should also be given to the levels of experience, knowledge, responsibility, and risk tolerance of both the seller and the buyer. For instance, if the seller lacks extensive experience in international trade and transportation arrangements, opting for an Incoterms with minimal responsibilities and associated risks (e.g. EXW) or confining arrangements and risks within the seller's country (e.g. FCA, FAS, FOB) is advisable.

Furthermore, the desired level of control over the shipping process must be determined by both parties. For instance, if the buyer has reliable logistics partners, they may prefer to handle transportation themselves to have more control over carrier selection, costs, routing, and insurance.

Assessment of the risks each party is willing to bear and the extent of obligations they can fulfil is essential. For example, if the seller wishes to avoid being at risk after handing over the goods for carriage until loading onto the vessel, the seller should avoid using CFR or CIF and instead opt for CPT, or CIP, where the risk transfers upon handing over to the carrier. Similarly, if the seller aims to avoid risks associated with the import customs process in the buyer's country, they should refrain from using DDP.

It is important to be aware that the obligation to clear goods for export and import extends beyond operational tasks and costs. It is also crucial to determine whether the seller or the buyer will bear the risk when difficulties arise. It is advisable for the party domiciled in the country of export or import, or one with a reliable local agent or representative there, to undertake the clearance process.

Clearly and explicitly indicate any special requests. Concerning special requests, additional obligations, or clarifications within the sales contract, it is of utmost importance to articulate them clearly and explicitly. For instance, although the seller has no obligation for loading under EXW, it is not uncommon for the seller to assist with loading operations. This can be specified with a clause such as 'the seller is obligated to load the goods onto the vehicle arranged by the buyer at the seller's premise'. Regarding unloading costs at the destination port under CFR and CIF terms, the buyer typically bears these expenses. However, in certain carriage contracts, freight charges may already include unloading charges from the vessel. To prevent double payment, it is advisable for the buyer to stipulate in the sales contract that unloading charges are the seller's responsibility.

It is important to note that Incoterms CIP and CIF impose the obligation to insure freight on the seller, with different coverage requirements. Under CIP, the seller must insure the goods for the buyer's benefit with Institute Cargo Clauses (A), whereas CIF requires insurance with Institute Cargo Clauses (C). Adjustments to insurance requirements, such as needing insurance Clauses (A) for CIF or Clauses (C) for CIP, can be agreed upon by both parties but must be explicitly stated in the sales contract to avoid potential legal disputes.

Conclusion

A thorough understanding of Incoterms is essential for managing the complexities of international trade. By clearly outlining how costs, responsibilities, and risks are divided between exporters and importers, Incoterms establish a standardised framework that reduces uncertainty and misinterpretation in trade contracts. They provide clarity on each party's obligations, ensuring transparency and mutual agreement before shipment.

The correct application of these terms influences several critical aspects of international transactions. Pricing strategies are shaped by the costs that the seller must bear. Logistics planning becomes more efficient, as responsibilities for different stages of transport are clearly defined. Insurance coverage is aligned with the exact point where risk transfers, while overall risk management benefits from knowing precisely when the buyer assumes liability for the goods. By offering a universally recognised commercial language, Incoterms not only prevent misunderstandings and costly disputes but also safeguard business relationships and enhance operational efficiency in cross-border trade.

However, defining responsibilities under Incoterms is only one part of ensuring a smooth international transaction. Once the delivery obligations are agreed upon, another critical step is complying with export–import customs formalities. These procedures, along with proper product classification under the HS and accurate documentation preparation, are essential for lawful and efficient cross-border trade.

In the following chapter, we will examine how customs formalities uphold national and international obligations, explore the HS system for product classification, and identify the key documents required to facilitate seamless trade. In short, while Incoterms clarify who does what, customs formalities ensure that trade flows legally and efficiently across borders.

Key Takeaway

1 Incoterms provide a standardised set of international rules that define the responsibilities of sellers and buyers, outlining who bears which costs and when risk transfers from sellers to buyers.
2 Incoterms create a common language for international trade, helping minimise misunderstandings and prevent disputes.
3 The chosen Incoterms significantly affect pricing, logistics, and risk management.
4 Incoterms are not a substitute for a full sales contract; they do not address ownership transfer, payment terms, product specifications, liability for non-conformity, or dispute resolution.

Notes

1 Pre-carriage is the initial stage of transportation, involving the movement of goods from the seller's location to the point where they will be handed over for the main carriage. It typically includes transportation from the seller's warehouse to a port, airport, or freight terminal.
2 Main carriage involves the transportation of goods across borders. It includes the movement of goods by sea, air, rail, or road from the initial point of departure to the destination country or port.
3 On-carriage is the final stage of transportation, where goods are moved from the destination port or terminal to the buyer's premises or another specified location. It involves the transportation of goods from the port of entry to the final destination.
4 The Incoterms Rules are protected by copyright owned by ICC. Further information on the Incoterms Rules may be obtained from the ICC website (https://iccwbo.org/). Incoterms and the Incoterms 2020 logo are trademarks of ICC. Use of these trademarks does not imply association with, approval of, or sponsorship by ICC unless specifically stated earlier.
5 ICC's official website: https://iccwbo.org/
6 Exporting products from the seller's country to the buyer's country typically involves a range of costs, including export packaging, pre-carriage, main carriage,

and on-carriage transportation. Additional expenses also arise from export and import customs formalities, port or terminal handling charges, loading and unloading fees at various stages, as well as the cost of insurance to cover potential risks during transit.

7 For further details, see International Chamber of Commerce. (n.d.-a). *Incoterms rules history*. https://iccwbo.org/business-solutions/incoterms-rules/incoterms-rules-history

8 Incoterms are a foundational element of international trade, defining the responsibilities of buyers and sellers in cross-border transactions. Resources on Incoterms range from the official rules published by the ICC (available on its official websites and in publications, e.g., ICC, 2019a, 2019b, 2022), to legal and academic commentaries (e.g., Piltz, 2020a, 2020b, 2021; ACERIS Law, 2020), international business texts (e.g., Seyoum, 2021; Capela, 2015), and industry-oriented tools and explanations provided by logistics firms and trade professionals (e.g., DHL, n.d.; Kuehne+Nagel, n.d.; SMP Global, n.d.; Trade Finance Global, 2025; Thompson, 2025). These diverse sources underscore the central role of Incoterms in enhancing legal clarity, commercial efficiency, and logistical coordination in global trade operations.

9 International Chamber of Commerce (ICC). (2019). *Incoterms 2020: ICC rules for the use of domestic and international trade terms*. ICC Publication, pp. 27–28.

10 The Institute Cargo Clauses (ICC) A, B, and C are commonly utilised within marine cargo insurance policies, each providing distinct levels of coverage.

Institute Cargo Clauses (C) is a required insurance under CIF Incoterms. The seller has the obligation to provide cargo insurance against the buyer's risk of loss or damage to the goods from the point of delivery to, at least, the port of destination. ICC (C) covers the narrowest scope of protection of loss or damage resulting from fire or explosion, ship grounding or sinking, collisions, overturning or derailment of land conveyances, cargo discharge at a port of distress, and general average sacrifice or jettison.

Institute Cargo Clauses (B) encompasses all aspects of ICC (C), additionally covering loss or damage reasonably attributed to earthquakes, volcanic eruptions, lightning, washing overboard, entry of sea water into the ship/container, and items dropped or lost overboard during loading and unloading.

Institutes Cargo Clauses (A) offers the broadest coverage, termed as "all risks", including loss or damage from malicious acts, theft, pilferage, non-delivery of the entire shipping package, piracy, and rainwater. However, despite its "all risks" nature, exceptions exist, such as wilful misconduct by the insured, inadequate packing, and inherent vice. ICC (A) is a required cargo insurance under CIP Incoterms. The seller has the obligation to contract for insurance to cover the risk of cargo loss or damage during transportation from the place of delivery to, at least, the place of destination.

For additional reading on related risk allocation and cargo coverage in international trade, see:

- London Market Association (LMA) for a detailed reference on Institute Cargo Clauses A, B and C. https://www.lmalloyds.com/lma/underwriting/marine/JCC/JCC_Clauses_Project/Cargo_Clauses.aspx
- Comparison of Institute Cargo Clauses (A), (B), and (C) by MSIG for an overview of coverage differences under standard marine insurance clauses, which often complement the risk obligations outlined in Incoterms. https://www.msig.com.hk/sites/msig_hk/files/Cover%20comparison%20between%20ICC%20%28A%29%28B%29%28C%29%20_1.pdf

11 This term represents a new feature of the 2020 Incoterms. DPU has replaced the DAT (Delivered at Terminal) term from the 2010 version, which had itself replaced the DEQ (Delivered ex Quay) term from the 2000 Incoterms.

9

CUSTOMS FORMALITIES PROCESS

Learning Objectives

1 Understand the purpose and importance of the customs formalities process.
2 Understand the structure and functions of the HS in classifying goods for international commerce.
3 Identify key documents typically required for the customs formalities process.

The Hidden Complexity Behind Customs Formalities

Every day, thousands of containers move across borders carrying diverse goods, such as electronics, rice, medical devices, and apparel. Have you ever wondered how customs authorities know what's inside? Who verifies that the shipment is legal, safe, and correctly taxed?

Customs formalities are the regulatory backbone of international trade, safeguarding sovereignty, security, and compliant cross-border commerce. For governments, they ensure proper revenue collection, enforcement of health and safety regulations, and protection of national interests. For example, strict customs checks prevent counterfeited products from entering a country. However, customs authorities do more than just inspect goods, and their work relies on a highly structured and internationally standardised product classification system, known as the Harmonized System. This framework makes it possible to track and regulate the movement of millions of products worldwide.

DOI: 10.4324/9781003535874-13

In international trade, accurate product classification is not merely for data recording. It plays a pivotal role in determining applicable tariff rates, legal compliance, and whether a product is subject to import/export licenses or permits. It ensures that shipments are handled lawfully, that governments can enforce health, safety, and environmental standards, and that global trade flows remain orderly and accountable.

For companies, customs formalities and correct HS classification are not just paperwork. They are a strategic necessity. A single misclassified shipment can lead to unexpected tariffs, costly delays, or even seizure of goods. In contrast, accurate classification ensures the correct tariff rates are applied, legal requirements are met, and shipments flow smoothly across borders.

What Is the Customs Formalities Process?

Customs formalities are the mandatory requirements that must be met to comply with customs regulations when goods cross international borders. These include both export customs formalities (in the country of export) and import customs formalities (in the country of import), and may include documentary requirements, security measures, information disclosure, physical inspections, and duty and tax payments.

These formalities are necessary to facilitate, regulate, and control the flow of goods across national borders, ensure compliance with customs laws and regulations. It is important to note that customs formalities and procedures can vary significantly from one country to another, so it is essential to be well-informed about the specific requirements of the country in which goods are exported or imported. Non-compliance with customs formalities can lead to penalties, fines, or legal actions.

An efficient customs formalities process can significantly enhance a country's competitiveness in the global marketplace. Countries with streamlined customs procedures are more attractive for conducting international trade and attracting foreign investment. Predictable and efficient customs processes reduce risks and uncertainties associated with cross-border trade, making it easier for businesses to invest in and operate within the country. Efficient customs processes reduce the time it takes for goods to move in and out of a country. Reduced delays at customs checkpoints translate into cost savings for businesses (WCO, 2023). Singapore, for example, has invested heavily in technology and streamlined customs procedures to make the process as efficient as possible. Most customs procedures can be completed electronically, reducing paperwork and delays, making the port of Singapore one of the world's busiest and most efficient ports. Table 9.1 presents the time required for export and import processes in selected countries.

TABLE 9.1 Time required for export and import processes in selected countries.

Economy	*Time to export: Border Compliance (hours)*	*Time to export: Documentary Compliance (hours)*	*Time to Import: Border Compliance (hours)*	*Time to Import: Documentary Compliance (hours)*
OECD High-income	12.7	2.3	8.5	3.4
Singapore	10	2	33	3
China (Shanghai)	18	8	37	11
India (Mumbai)	50	18	60	22

Source: World Bank (n.d.-f)

The customs formalities process typically involves:

Declaration of goods: The declarant must complete a customs declaration form, providing detailed information about the goods being imported or exported. This declaration includes information about the nature, quantity, value, and origin of the goods[1] and also involves customs documentation. This can include commercial invoices, packing lists, bills of lading (B/L), certificates of origin, and other relevant permits and licenses.

Goods examination: Non-intrusive methods, such as X-ray scanning or container scanning, may be used to examine the contents of containers or shipments without physically opening them. However, customs authorities may physically inspect goods to verify the accuracy of the declaration and assess their condition. They also ensure compliance with the declaration form, other required customs documentation, import or export restrictions, applicable laws, as well as health and safety standards.

Assessment and collection of customs duties and taxes: At this stage, customs authorities assess the classification of goods under the HS codes to determine the applicable customs duties and ensure compliance with the country's import/export regulations.

Customs clearance and release of goods: Once customs duties and taxes are paid and all customs formalities are completed, goods are released to enter the country. If customs formalities are not completed, or if discrepancies or non-compliance are detected, the goods may be detained for further inspection and potential legal action. In severe cases, goods may be confiscated or destroyed.

Record keeping and post-clearance review: Customs authorities maintain records of import and export transactions for data collection and audit. Customs authorities may conduct post-clearance audits or reviews to ensure that customs duties and taxes were assessed correctly and that all regulations were followed.

Prohibited Goods versus Restricted Goods

Customs offices play a vital role in facilitating trade while safeguarding national security, public health, safety, and the environment through the customs formalities process. Goods that pose such risks are regulated by governments and are classified as either prohibited or restricted. It is important to be aware that customs regulations regarding prohibited and restricted goods vary from country to country. Consequently, an item deemed permissible in one country may be subject to restrictions or outright bans in another. Compliance with country-specific customs regulations is therefore essential to avoid legal and administrative penalties in cross-border transactions.

Prohibited Goods

Prohibited goods are items that are completely banned from import or export, meaning they cannot legally enter or leave a country under any circumstances. Examples include items that pose a threat to national security, or goods that could harm public health or safety, such as illegal drugs and counterfeit medications. However, what is considered prohibited varies from country to country, depending on national laws, cultural values, and public safety concerns.

For example, in Singapore, prohibited goods include chewing gum (except for therapeutic or dental purposes), pistol- or revolver-shaped cigarette lighters, and telephone voice-changing equipment.[2] According to Abu Dhabi Customs in the United Arab Emirates (UAE), prohibited goods include publications, photographs, oil paintings, books, magazines, and sculptures that violate Islamic principles or public morals, or are intended as pornography; three-layer nylon fishing nets; asbestos boards and pipes; and laser pens with red flashlight beams.[3] In South Africa, prohibited goods include prison-made goods, narcotic and habit-forming drugs in any form, weapons, explosives, fireworks, and toxic substances such as poisons.[4]

Restricted Goods

In contrast, restricted goods are items that may be imported or exported only if specific conditions are met, such as obtaining a permit, license, or meeting strict regulatory requirements. These goods are not completely prohibited, but their movement is tightly controlled to ensure safety, security, or compliance with relevant legal and regulatory requirements.

For instance, Singapore's restricted goods include military equipment such as tanks, marine vessels, guns, aircraft, and bombs, as well as dual-use goods like nuclear materials, electronic components, telecommunications equipment, sensors, lasers, and navigation systems. South Africa's restricted goods include used goods, waste, discarded materials, ashes, and remnants. Meanwhile, Abu

Dhabi Customs (UAE) restricts live animals and their products, alcoholic beverages, fuel, cosmetics, blood, and raw diamonds.

What Is the Harmonized System (HS)?

The HS, developed by the WCO, is an internationally standardised system for classifying and categorising goods and products traded across borders. Its primary purpose is to facilitate international trade and customs operations by providing a universally recognised method for classifying and describing goods. In other words, HS is a uniform classification, a globally accepted framework for classifying products consistently across countries. This uniformity is essential for international trade and customs procedures to ensure that products are categorised in the same way worldwide.

The HS code is used to determine the applicable customs duties, taxes, and tariffs when goods are imported or exported. Each code corresponds to a specific tariff rate, enabling customs authorities to accurately calculate duties and taxes. HS codes are an essential part of trade agreements and appear on key customs and shipping documents, including invoices, B/L, and customs declarations. This universal classification system enables customs officials to quickly identify and clear goods during inspections and clearance procedures. Additionally, HS codes serve an important statistical function: governments and international organisations use them to compile trade data, track the volume and value of traded goods, and analyse global trade patterns and trends.

The WCO has revised and updated HS codes periodically (1988, 1996, 2002, 2007, 2012, 2017, 2022) to reflect changes in global trade and product innovation. With each change, some HS codes are removed, others have changes to their definitions, with some definitions expanding to include more goods. The latest HS 2022 is the seventh edition of the HS nomenclature, which has entered into force since January 1, 2022. More than 200 countries worldwide use the HS code system to classify goods in international trade, covering more than 98% of global trade flows (WCO, n.d.-a, n.d.-b, n.d.-c).

The HS 2022 comprises approximately 5,300 product descriptions organised into headings and subheadings, which are structured across 97 chapters[5] and grouped into 21 sections. Table 9.2 presents the HS 2022 sections, chapters, and a brief description of each chapter.

Structure of the HS Code

The HS code follows a hierarchical structure that allows for the systematic classification of traded goods, moving from broad categories (section and chapter) to more specific levels (heading, subheading, and national tariff line). Each product category is assigned a unique numerical code. At the international level, HS codes consist of six digits, while individual countries may extend

TABLE 9.2 HS 2022 sections code list.[6]

Section	*Chapter*	*Chapter Description*
Section I: Live Animals; Animal Products	1	Live animals
	2	Meat and edible meat offal
	3	Fish and crustaceans, molluscs, and other aquatic invertebrates
	4	Dairy produce; birds' eggs; natural honey; edible products of animal origin, not elsewhere specified or included
	5	Products of animal origin, not elsewhere specified or included
Section II: Vegetable Products	6	Live trees and other plants; bulbs, roots, and the like; cut flowers and ornamental foliage
	7	Edible vegetables and certain roots and tubers
	8	Edible fruit and nuts; peel of citrus fruit or melons
	9	Coffee, tea, maté, and spices
	10	Cereals
	11	Products of the milling industry, malt, starches, inulin, wheat gluten
	12	Oil seeds and oleaginous fruits; miscellaneous grains, seeds, and fruit; industrial or medicinal plants; straw and fodder
	13	Lac; gums, resins, and other vegetable saps and extracts
	14	Vegetable plaiting materials; vegetable products not elsewhere specified or included
Section III: Animal or Vegetable Fats and Oils	15	Animal or vegetable fats and oils and their cleavage products; prepared edible fats; animal or vegetable waxes
Section IV: Prepared Foodstuffs	16	Preparations of meat, of fish, or of crustaceans, molluscs, or other aquatic invertebrates
	17	Sugars and sugar confectionery
	18	Cocoa and cocoa preparations
	19	Preparations of cereals, flour, starch, or milk; pastrycooks' products
	20	Preparations of vegetables, fruit, nuts, or other parts of plants
	21	Miscellaneous edible preparations
	22	Beverages, spirits, and vinegar
	23	Residues and waste from the food industries, prepared animal fodder
	24	Tobacco and manufactured tobacco substitutes

(*Continued*)

TABLE 9.2 (Continued)

Section	*Chapter*	*Chapter Description*
Section V: Mineral Products	25	Salt; sulphur; earths and stone; plastering materials, lime, and cement
	26	Ores, slag, and ash
	27	Mineral fuels, mineral oils, and products of their distillation; bituminous substances; mineral waxes
Section VI: Chemical Products	28	Inorganic chemicals; organic or inorganic compounds of precious metals, of rare-earth metals, of radioactive elements, or of isotopes
	29	Organic chemicals
	30	Pharmaceutical products
	31	Fertilisers
	32	Tanning or dyeing extracts; tannins and their derivatives; dyes, pigments, and other colouring matter; paints and varnishes; putty and other mastics; inks
	33	Essential oils and resinoids; perfumery and cosmetic or toilet preparations
	34	Soap, organic surface-active agents, washing preparations, lubricating preparations, artificial waxes, prepared waxes, polishing or scouring preparations, candles and similar articles, modelling pastes, 'dental waxes', and dental preparations
	35	Albuminoidal substances; modified starches; glues; enzymes
	36	Explosives; pyrotechnic products; matches; pyrophoric alloys; certain combustible preparations
	37	Photographic or cinematographic goods
	38	Miscellaneous chemical products
Section VII: Plastics and Articles Thereof	39	Plastics and articles thereof
	40	Rubber and articles thereof
Section VIII: Raw Hides and Skins, Leather, Fur Skins	41	Raw hides and skins (other than fur skins) and leather
	42	Articles of leather; saddlery and harness; travel goods, handbags, and similar containers; articles of animal gut (other than silk-worm gut)
	43	Fur skins and artificial fur; manufactures thereof

(*Continued*)

TABLE 9.2 (Continued)

Section	*Chapter*	*Chapter Description*
Section IX: Wood and Articles of Wood	44	Wood and articles of wood; wood charcoal
	45	Cork and articles of cork
	46	Manufactures of straw, of esparto, or of other plaiting materials; basket-ware and wickerwork
Section X: Pulp of Wood, Paper, and Paperboard	47	Pulp of wood or of other fibrous cellulosic material; recovered (waste and scrap) paper or paperboard
	48	Paper and paperboard; articles of paper pulp, of paper, or of paperboard
	49	Printed books, newspapers, pictures, and other products of the printing industry; manuscripts, typescripts, and plans
Section XI: Textiles and Textile Articles	50	Silk
	51	Wool, fine or coarse animal hair; horsehair yarn; and woven fabric
	52	Cotton
	53	Other vegetable textile fibres; paper yarn and woven fabrics of paper yarn
	54	Man-made filaments, strip, and the like of man-made textile materials
	55	Man-made staple fibres
	56	Wadding, felt, and non-wovens; special yarns; twine, cordage, ropes, cables, and articles thereof
	57	Carpets and other textile floor coverings
	58	Special woven fabrics; tufted textile fabrics; lace; tapestries; trimmings; embroidery
	59	Impregnated, coated, covered, or laminated textile fabrics; textile articles of a kind suitable for industrial use
	60	Knitted or crocheted fabrics
	61	Articles of apparel and clothing accessories, knitted or crocheted
	62	Articles of apparel and clothing accessories, not knitted or crocheted
	63	Other made-up textile articles; sets; worn clothing and worn textile articles; rags

(*Continued*)

TABLE 9.2 (Continued)

Section	*Chapter*	*Chapter Description*
Section XII: Footwear, Headgear, Umbrellas, etc.	64	Footwear, gaiters, and the like; parts of such articles
	65	Headgear and parts thereof
	66	Umbrellas, sun umbrellas, walking sticks, seat-sticks, whips, riding-crops, and parts thereof
	67	Prepared feathers and down and articles made of feathers or of down; artificial flowers; articles of human hair
Section XIII: Articles of Stone, Ceramic, Glass	68	Articles of stone, plaster, cement, asbestos, mica, or similar materials
	69	Ceramic products
	70	Glass and glassware
Section XIV: Natural or Cultured Pearls, Precious Metals	71	Natural or cultured pearls, precious or semi-precious stones, precious metals, metals clad with precious metal, and articles thereof; imitation jewellery; coin
Section XV: Base Metals and Articles of Base Metal	72	Iron and steel
	73	Articles of iron or steel
	74	Copper and articles thereof
	75	Nickel and articles thereof
	76	Aluminium and articles thereof
	77	Reserved for possible future use in the HS
	78	Lead and articles thereof
	79	Zinc and articles thereof
	80	Tin and articles thereof
	81	Other base metals; cermets; articles thereof
	82	Tools, implements, cutlery, spoons, and forks, of base metal; parts thereof of base metal
	83	Miscellaneous articles of base metal
Section XVI: Machinery and Electrical Equipment	84	Nuclear reactors, boilers, machinery, and mechanical appliances; parts thereof
	85	Electrical machinery and equipment and parts thereof; sound recorders and reproducers, television image and sound recorders and reproducers, and parts and accessories of such articles

(*Continued*)

TABLE 9.2 (Continued)

Section	*Chapter*	*Chapter Description*
Section XVII: Vehicles, Aircraft, Vessels	86	Railway or tramway locomotives, rolling stock and parts thereof; railway or tramway track fixtures and fittings and parts thereof; mechanical (including electro-mechanical) traffic signalling equipment of all kinds
	87	Vehicles other than railway or tramway rolling stock and parts and accessories thereof
	88	Aircraft, spacecraft, and parts thereof
	89	Ships, boats, and floating structures
Section XVIII: Optical, Photographic Instruments	90	Optical, photographic, cinematographic, measuring, checking, precision, medical, or surgical instruments and apparatus; parts and accessories thereof
	91	Clocks and watches and parts thereof
	92	Musical instruments; parts and accessories of such articles
Section XIX: Arms and Ammunition	93	Arms and ammunition; parts and accessories thereof
Section XX: Miscellaneous Manufactured Articles	94	Furniture; bedding, mattresses, mattress supports, cushions and similar stuffed furnishings; lamps and lighting fittings, not elsewhere specified or included; illuminated signs, illuminated nameplates, and the like; prefabricated buildings
	95	Toys, games, and sports requisites; parts and accessories thereof
	96	Miscellaneous manufactured articles
Section XXI: Works of Art, Collectors' Pieces	97	Works of art, collectors' pieces, and antiques

Source: WCO (n.d.-b).

them with additional digits to meet their own tariff and statistical requirements. This layered structure enables classification at varying levels of detail, from general product groups to highly specific goods. Figure 9.1 illustrates the structure of the Harmonized System (HS) code.

For example, Hom Mali rice[7] is classified under HS code 1006.30.40.000. At the broadest level, it falls under Section II, Vegetable Products, and more specifically, Chapter 10, Cereals. Within this chapter, Heading 1006 refers to rice, while Subheading 1006.30 narrows it further to semi-milled or wholly milled rice, whether or not polished or glazed. At the national level in Thailand, the code is extended to 1006.30.40, which specifically identifies jasmine rice (Hom Mali), and finally 1006.30.40.000 becomes the complete national

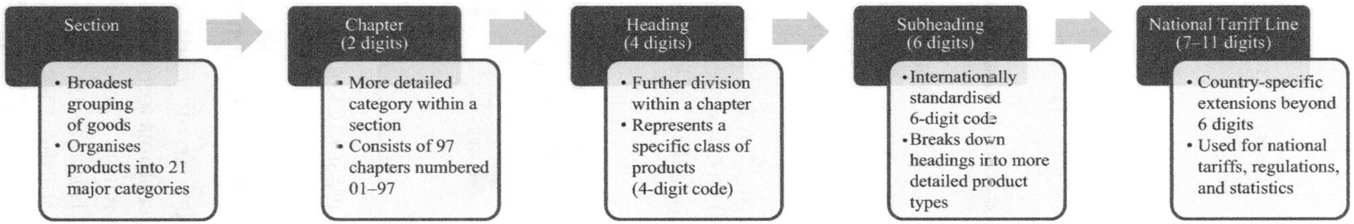

FIGURE 9.1 Structure of the Harmonized System (HS) code.

tariff line used for tariff and statistical purposes. The HS code structure for Hom Mali rice is shown in Figure 9.2.

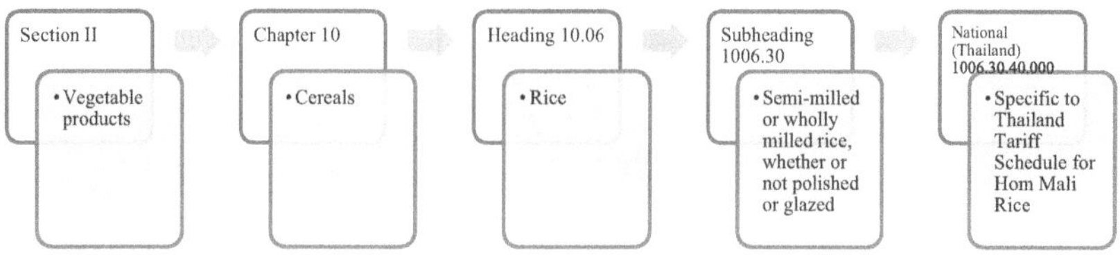

FIGURE 9.2 HS code structure for Hom Mali rice.

Similarly, a laptop computer is classified under HS code 8471.30.0100. It starts broadly under Section XVI, Machinery and Mechanical Appliances; Electrical Equipment, and is placed in Chapter 84, Machinery and Mechanical Appliances. Within this chapter, Heading 8471 covers automatic data-processing machines, while Subheading 8471.30 narrows it to portable automatic data-processing machines weighing not more than 10 kg. At the national level in the United States, 8471.30.01 identifies laptop computers specifically, and 8471.30.0100 is the complete tariff line for laptops.[8] Figure 9.3 shows the HS code structure of laptop computers.

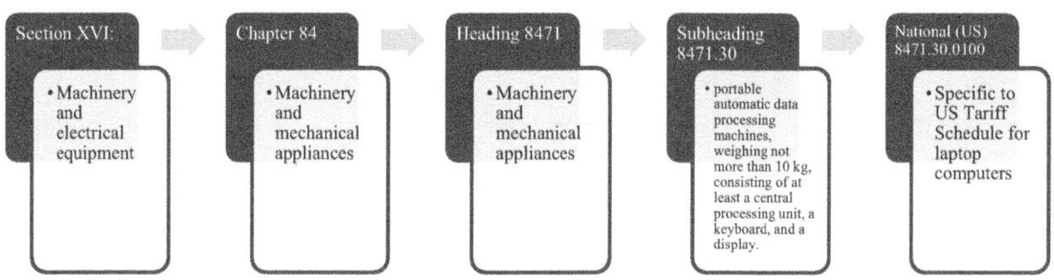

FIGURE 9.3 HS code structure for laptop computers.

Key Documents for Export and Import Customs Formalities

The efficient and lawful movement of goods across international borders depends on a structured set of customs formalities designed to ensure regulatory compliance and safeguard national security. At the core of these formalities lies a critical component of trade documentation.

Trade documents serve as the formal bridge between businesses and customs authorities, enabling officials to verify shipments, determine the correct duties and taxes, and authorise the entry or exit of goods. Beyond facilitating customs clearance, these documents play multiple roles, including supporting customs valuation, enabling transportation tracking, substantiating insurance claims, and legally validating the transaction. While the exact documentation required may vary depending on the type of goods, the destination country, and any applicable trade agreements, certain key documents are universally important in the customs clearance process. The following documents are among the most commonly required.

Commercial invoice: In international trade, a commercial invoice is one of the most fundamental and legally significant documents in a cross-border transaction. It acts as the official record of sale between the exporter (seller) and the importer (buyer) and serves multiple legal, financial, and customs-related purposes.

A commercial invoice details key transaction information, including names and addresses of the exporter and importer, description of goods (type, quantity, unit price), HS code, total value of goods and currency used, terms of sale (e.g. Incoterms such as FOB, CIF), payment terms, shipment details (date, method, port of loading and discharge), and other key sale conditions.

A commercial invoice serves as proof of the transaction between the buyer and seller. In the customs clearance process, it is the primary document used by customs authorities in both the exporting and importing countries to assess product classification, duties and taxes, and compliance with export and import regulations. Errors or missing information can lead to clearance delays, fines, or cargo seizure.

Moreover, when a letter of credit or a documentary collection is used, the commercial invoice is a required document to trigger payment. Banks use it to verify that goods match the conditions of the trade finance agreement. Insurance companies use it to determine coverage and premiums. The commercial invoice also serves as proof of value for insurance claims in case of damage or loss.

Packing list: A packing list is a document prepared by the exporter or freight forwarder that details the physical contents of a shipment. It details how products are packed, itemises the contents of each package, and specifies the number, size, and weight of packages. This information is indispensable for freight forwarders, carriers, and warehouse operators to plan cargo loading, stacking, and routing effectively, optimise transport space, and reduce the likelihood of damage or misplacement.

Customs authorities in both the exporting and importing countries rely on the export packing list to verify the physical contents of a shipment against accompanying documents, such as the commercial invoice and B/L. Accurate packing lists help expedite customs inspections and reduce the risk of delays, fines, or cargo holds due to discrepancies or incomplete declarations.

For importers, the packing list is an essential tool for verifying incoming goods upon arrival. It supports efficient inventory management by providing a detailed breakdown of items, quantities, and packaging configurations. In cases of cargo damage or loss during transit, the packing list enables importers to identify missing or affected goods and serves as supporting evidence in insurance claims. It allows insurers to determine the nature, value, and condition of the goods, as well as the number and state of packages prior to shipment.

Transport documents: Transport documents are issued by the carrier and vary by mode of transport.

A bill of lading (B/L) is a legally binding transport document issued by an ocean carrier to the shipper. It serves three primary functions. First, it serves as a receipt of goods, confirming that the carrier has received the cargo. Second, it serves as a contract of carriage, outlining the terms and responsibilities for transporting the goods. Third, it serves as a document of title. The holder of the original B/L has legal ownership and control of the cargo. B/L is an important document, as it is required to release goods to the buyer or consignee.

An air waybill (AWB) is a transport document issued by an airline. It serves as a receipt of goods for air transport, a contract of carriage, and proof of shipment.

Road/rail consignment note is a transport document used for land freight. It serves as a receipt of goods from the consignor, a contract of carriage between the consignor and carrier, and evidence of the carrier's obligation to deliver the goods to the named consignee.

Certificate of Origin (CO): A certificate of origin is an official document that verifies the country where goods were manufactured or produced. It serves as proof of origin for exported goods and is often required by customs authorities in the importing country to determine tariff eligibility under FTAs.

Import/Export Licenses or Permits: An import/export license or permit is an official authorisation granted by a government agency that allows a business or individual to legally import or export restricted or controlled goods. These licenses are instruments for the government to control sensitive goods (e.g. arms, ammunition, defence items); protect public health and safety (e.g. pharmaceuticals and medical equipment, hazardous chemicals, and waste); fulfil international agreements (e.g. CITES, dual-use controls[9]); or enforce trade quotas, sanctions, or embargoes.

In addition to the documents discussed above, other documents may be required depending on the nature of the product and the specific legal requirements of the exporting and importing countries. For example, *a phytosanitary certificate* is essential for plant and plant-based products, confirming they are free from pests and diseases.[10] *A health certificate* is required for food products to ensure they meet the importing country's food safety standards. *A certificate with respect to meat* may be specifically required to certify the origin, safety, and handling of meat products in accordance with veterinary and public health regulations. For food products intended for Muslim markets – such as Indonesia, Malaysia, or Saudi Arabia – *a halal certificate* is mandatory to confirm that the products conform to Islamic dietary laws and are processed according to certified halal standards.[11]

These required documents, though varying across jurisdictions, are essential for ensuring that traded goods comply with the legal, health, and security requirements. Staying informed about the latest customs requirements in both the exporting and importing countries is therefore critical. Failure to do so can result in shipment delays, additional costs, confiscation, or even destruction of goods. Equally important is clearly identifying which party (typically the exporter) is responsible for preparing and providing specific documents. This responsibility should always be explicitly stated in the sales contract to prevent misunderstandings and avoid costly complications.

Conclusion

Customs formalities form an essential foundation of cross-border trade, ensuring the lawful and efficient movement of goods between nations. For governments, these procedures are a vital mechanism to facilitate and regulate trade flows. For businesses, customs formalities are a strategic element of global supply chain management, as they directly influence costs, delivery timelines, and speed to market. Central to these procedures is the accurate classification of goods under the HS code, which determines applicable tariff rates, supports statistical reporting, and ensures compliance with trade regulations. Companies must stay well-informed about customs requirements in both the exporting and importing countries to avoid costly delays or penalties. Equally important is the preparation of accurate and complete trade documentation, which serves as the legal and operational backbone of any cross-border shipment.

In the next chapter, we will move from customs formalities to examine the key contracts underpinning international trade, including sales contracts, carriage contracts, insurance contracts, and L/C contracts. We will explore how these agreements create specific obligations, how they work together to safeguard transactions, and how disputes arising from them can be effectively resolved.

Key Takeaway

1. Customs formalities are a critical element of international trade. They are the official procedures and requirements that goods must undergo when crossing international borders to ensure compliance with the laws and regulations of both the exporting and importing countries.
2. Accurate classification of goods using the HS code is essential, as it determines regulatory requirements, applicable tariff rates, and facilitates statistical reporting.
3. Certain products are restricted, require special licenses, or are outright prohibited due to health, safety, environmental, or national security concerns. Firms must stay informed about these requirements to avoid legal risks and ensure smooth customs clearance.
4. Trade documentation forms the legal and operational backbone of cross-border shipments. Accurate and complete documents facilitate customs clearance, support insurance claims and trade financing, and serve as proof of compliance with regulatory and contractual obligations.
5. Countries that streamline, digitalise, and modernise customs processes create a more trade-friendly environment, attracting investment and enhancing competitiveness. On the business side, firms that master customs requirements gain a strategic advantage by managing costs, reducing lead times, and improving market access.

Notes

1 As an example, see details of Japan's procedure for import/export declaration at Japan Customs. (n.d.-b). https://www.customs.go.jp/english/procedures/index_pf.htm

Articles prohibited from importation/exportation are shown at Japan Customs. (n.d.-a). https://www.customs.go.jp/english/c-answer_e/customsanswer_e.htm#kinsei

2 Further information on Singapore's controlled and prohibited goods for import can be found at https://www.customs.gov.sg/businesses/importing-goods/controlled-and-prohibited-goods-for-import/ and https://www.dhl.com/discover/en-sg/ship-with-dhl/essential-guides/understanding-the-differences-between-strategic-prohibited-and-restricted-goods

3 Further information on Abu Dhabi's restricted and prohibited goods can be found at Abu Dhabi Customs. (n.d.). https://www.adcustoms.gov.ae/en/Restricted-Banned-Commodities

4 Further information on South Africa's prohibited and restricted imports can be found at International Trade Administration. (n.d.). https://www.trade.gov/country-commercial-guides/south-africa-prohibited-and-restricted-imports

5 Although some sources mention 99 chapters in the Harmonized System (HS), the official HS Nomenclature administered by the WCO contains only 97 chapters. These chapters are numbered from 1 to 97 and are universally applied by all contracting parties to the HS Convention. The confusion surrounding the number

of chapters arises because some national customs authorities, such as the United States International Trade Commission (USITC), add Chapter 98 and Chapter 99 to accommodate temporary or special national provisions. For instance, Chapter 98 typically deals with special classification provisions like returned goods or personal exemptions, while Chapter 99 covers temporary legislation or trade remedies, including tariff rate quotas or retaliatory tariffs (USITC, 2024). However, these additional chapters are not part of the official HS maintained by the WCO. Therefore, while countries may expand their own tariff schedules for domestic purposes, the internationally recognised system includes only 97 chapters.

6 Details of HS Nomenclature 2022 edition can be accessed at WCO. (n.d.-b). https://www.wcoomd.org/en/topics/nomenclature/instrument-and-tools/hs-nomenclature-2022-edition/hs-nomenclature-2022-edition.aspx

7 Hom Mali rice, also known as Thai jasmine rice, is a premium, long-grain variety of fragrant rice that originates from Thailand. It is internationally renowned for its distinct aroma, soft texture, and slightly sweet flavour when cooked. Thailand holds geographical indication protection for 'Thai Hom Mali Rice', meaning authentic Hom Mali rice must be grown in specific regions of northeastern Thailand. For detailed of HS code, see Thai Customs Department. (n.d.). *Tariff nomenclature and HS classification database.* http://itd.customs.go.th/igtf/th/main_frame.jsp?lang=th&top_menu=menu_homepage&current_id=5028

8 For details on US Harmonized Tariff Schedule, see United States International Trade Commission. (2024). *Harmonized tariff schedule of the United States (2025).* https://hts.usitc.gov

9 The Convention on International Trade in Endangered Species of Wild Fauna and Flora (CITES) regulates the cross-border movement of endangered species and related products to ensure their protection through international trade controls. It is governed by the CITES Convention, signed in 1973 and administered by the CITES Secretariat under the United Nations Environment Programme (UNEP).

Dual-use control refers to regulatory measures governing the export, transit, and brokering of goods, software, and technologies that can be used for both civilian and military purposes. These controls are primarily guided by the Wassenaar Arrangement on Export Controls for Conventional Arms and Dual-Use Goods and Technologies (1996), as well as national and regional frameworks such as the European Union Dual-Use Regulation (EU) 2021/821.

10 The European Union imposes strict phytosanitary requirements on plants and plant products imported from non-EU countries. Under Regulation (EU) 2019/2072, items listed in Annex XI and Annex XII must be accompanied by a phytosanitary certificate confirming they are inspected and free from harmful pests. See European Commission. (n.d.-b). *Trade in plants & plant products from non-EU countries.*

11 Many Islamic countries require halal certification for the importation and sale of food, beverages, pharmaceuticals, and other consumables to ensure compliance with Islamic dietary laws. In Malaysia, for example, halal certification is administered by the Department of Islamic Development Malaysia (JAKIM), which outlines detailed procedures and standards in its *Manual Procedure for Malaysia Halal Certification (Third Revision)* (JAKIM, 2014).

10

KEY CONTRACTS IN INTERNATIONAL TRADE

Learning Objectives

1 Understand key contracts in international trade, including sales contracts, carriage contracts, cargo insurance contracts, and letters of credit.
2 Be able to explain the obligations inherent in each of these contracts.
3 Understand methods for resolving international trade disputes.

Agreed Terms, Defined Obligations

Imagine this scenario: Java Essence Co., an Indonesian coffee exporter, secures a deal to sell five tons of premium Sumatra coffee beans to a US importer for $50,000, under the trade term CIF Port of Los Angeles.

Java Essence ships the coffee, expecting smooth delivery and prompt payment.

When the shipment arrives in Los Angeles, the importer refuses to pay, alleging that the beans do not meet the agreed moisture level. The shipping company, responsible for transport, denies liability for the damage. The insurer also rejects the claim, arguing that improper packaging caused the problem. The bank refuses to release funds under the L/C, citing minor discrepancies in the shipping documents.

What seemed like a straightforward transaction spirals into a web of disputes. Each contract – the sales contract, the carriage contract, the insurance contract, and the L/C – binds different parties with separate obligations, making resolution complex, time-consuming, and costly.

DOI: 10.4324/9781003535874-14

In international trade, a single transaction often involves multiple parties working together to facilitate the movement of goods from one location to another. This complex process includes not only the buyer and seller but also carriers, banks, and others, all playing crucial roles throughout the export–import procedure. Various contracts are put in place to manage different aspects of the transaction, including a sales contract, which outlines the terms of the deal between the buyer and seller; a carriage contract, which ensures the transportation of goods across borders; a cargo insurance contract, which provide protection against loss or damage during transit; and an L/C, which secures payment between the buyer and seller. Each of these contracts binds different parties, each with specific obligations and responsibilities, ensuring that all aspects of the trade are properly managed and safeguarded.

To minimise risks, businesses must ensure their contracts are clear, comprehensive, and aligned, explicitly outlining obligations, liabilities, and dispute resolution mechanisms.

International Sales Contract

An international sales contract is a legally binding agreement that clearly defines the rights and obligations of the seller and the buyer in a cross-border transaction.

The seller is the party that agrees to supply and deliver goods to the buyer as per the agreed terms. Their obligations typically include manufacturing or sourcing the goods, ensuring that the goods comply with agreed quality and specifications, and packing and labelling according to international trade requirements. However, their obligations can extend to arranging transportation, providing necessary export documentation, and managing the customs formality process, depending on the agreed Incoterms.

The buyer is the party that agrees to purchase and pay for the goods under the agreed terms. Their obligations typically include paying for the goods as per contract terms. However, their obligations can also extend, depending on the agreed Incoterms.

Beyond simply outlining what is being sold and at what price, a sales contract provides a comprehensive framework that governs delivery, payment, risk allocation, and dispute resolution. A well-structured contract is essential not only for ensuring operational clarity and mutual understanding between the parties but also for safeguarding enforceability in case of non-performance, delays, or other disputes. In practices, such an international sales contract defines obligations between a buyer and a seller and is interlinked with multiple other contracts such as transportation, cargo insurance, and payment. Each of these related contracts must align with the terms of the sales agreement to ensure smooth execution of the transaction. A carriage contract ensures the goods are transported from the seller to the buyer, specifying the mode of transport and the responsibilities of the carrier. To safeguard against potential risks during transit, an insurance contract is often arranged to provide coverage for loss or damage. Meanwhile, a L/C secures payment by involving a financial institution that guarantees the buyer's obligation to pay, provided the seller meets the agreed requirements.

To illustrate, if an exporter and an importer agree to trade under FOB Incoterms, the seller fulfills their delivery obligation by placing the goods on board the vessel at the named port of shipment. This requires the seller to manage and pay for all logistics from their premises to the port, including inland transport, port handling, and ensuring the goods are loaded onto the agreed vessel on schedule.

On the other side, the buyer would be responsible for arranging transportation from the loading port to their premises. This could involve contracting with a shipping line, paying for ocean freight and unloading costs at the destination port, and arranging inland transportation to their warehouse.

Both parties must consider how to manage risks during transportation. The seller might want to insure the goods until they are loaded onto the vessel. After the goods have been loaded and the risk transfers to the buyer, the buyer may need to arrange insurance for the subsequent leg of the journey and any potential risk after the goods are transferred at the port of destination.

International sales contracts can be much more sophisticated than a domestic contract due to additional complexities that arise when transactions cross national borders. For example, a domestic sales contract is governed by a single country's commercial laws, whereas an international sales contract is subject to multiple legal frameworks as well as regulatory and compliance issues, including international conventions such as United Nations Convention on Contracts for the International Sale of Goods (CISG),[1] Incoterms, and national laws such as customs regulations, export–import controls, and product standards.

Payments for domestic sales are typically made in local currency with fewer concerns about currency fluctuations, whereas payment for international sales may involve L/C, D/C, or international money transfer. Foreign exchange fluctuations and capital control restrictions add complexity.

Transportation and logistics arrangement for domestic sales typically have fewer documentation requirements. International sales require detailed logistics planning and management, including export/import documentation (such as commercial invoice, B/L, CO, packing list, insurance certificate) and compliance with customs clearance procedures.

Domestic sales are subject solely to national taxation (e.g. local tax, VAT/GST), whereas international sales may involve import duties and taxes in the destination country.

Finally, while disputes in domestic sales contracts are typically settled in local courts under national laws, international sales contracts involve parties from different jurisdictions and, possibly, different legal systems. Consequently, it is essential that the buyer and seller agree upon the governing law, jurisdiction, and dispute resolution methods beforehand to ensure legal certainty[2].

Key components of an international sales contract include:

Identification of the Contracting Parties: The contract must begin by clearly identifying the seller and the buyer involved in the transaction, including their full legal names, official business addresses, and relevant contact details.

Description of the Goods: A comprehensive and unambiguous description of the goods is essential. This section should detail the product name, model or serial number, technical specifications, quantity, quality standards, and applicable packaging or labelling requirements. Clarity in this provision helps mitigate the risk of disputes related to product conformity or performance.

Packaging and Labelling Requirements: International shipments often require compliance with specific packaging and labelling standards. The contract should specify how the goods are to be packaged and labelled, particularly where regulatory requirements or handling instructions are involved. This provision is critical for ensuring safe transport, customs clearance, and legal compliance.

Price and Payment Terms: This section outlines the total price, the currency of settlement, the method of payment, and the timing of payment.

Delivery Terms: The delivery clause is commonly expressed through Incoterms. These terms clearly define the obligations of each party with regard to transportation costs, risk transfer, insurance, and customs formalities. Using Incoterms accurately is essential to prevent misunderstandings and ensure a clear allocation of costs and risks between the buyer and the seller.

Documentation Requirements: To ensure the smooth flow of goods and compliance with international regulations, the contract should clearly specify all required documents to be provided by the seller. These may include the commercial invoice, packing list, bill of lading or airway bill, certificate of origin, insurance certificate, and any others. A well defined documentation section ensures legal conformity, supports payment procedures, and facilitates efficient customs clearance.

Inspection and Acceptance Procedures: Provisions regarding the inspection and acceptance of goods help manage the risk of disputes over quality or conformity. The contract should outline the procedures for inspecting goods upon arrival, including timeframes, criteria for acceptance or rejection, and remedies available in the event of non-conforming goods.

Warranties and Guarantees: This clause defines any warranties or guarantees offered by the seller concerning the quality, durability, or performance of the goods. It should specify the scope and duration of the warranty, as well as the obligations of the seller in the event that the goods fail to meet agreed specifications.

Insurance Coverage: Where applicable, the contract should state whether the seller or the buyer is responsible for insuring the goods during transit. The scope and type of insurance should be clarified, particularly when required by Incoterms CIF and CIP.

Retention of Title (Reservation of Ownership): This clause stipulates when legal ownership of the goods is transferred from the seller to the buyer. A common provision allows the seller to retain title to the goods until full payment is received, thus providing an additional layer of security in credit-based transactions.

Force Majeure: A force majeure clause protects both parties from liability in the event that contractual obligations cannot be fulfilled due to unforeseeable and uncontrollable events, such as natural disasters, wars, pandemics, or government-imposed trade restrictions. The clause should define the types of events covered and outline the procedures for notification and mitigation.

Dispute Resolution, Governing Law, and Jurisdiction: Given the cross-border nature of international trade, the contract must specify the method for resolving disputes, whether through negotiation, mediation, arbitration, or litigation. Additionally, the contract should identify the applicable governing law (e.g. English law, US law, CISG) and the jurisdiction or venue where disputes will be adjudicated.

Termination Conditions: This section sets out the circumstances under which the contract may be terminated, including breaches of contract, insolvency, or mutual agreement. It should also outline the legal and financial consequences of termination, including return of goods, payment obligations, and potential claims for damages.

Confidentiality: Where sensitive information is exchanged – such as pricing structures, proprietary technology, or trade secrets – a confidentiality clause is advisable. This provision restricts the disclosure and use of such information to prevent competitive harm or legal exposure.

Compliance with Laws and Sanctions: Parties to an international sales contract must comply with all applicable export control laws, import regulations, and international sanctions. To ensure adherence to these requirements, the contract should include an explicit compliance clause to affirm that neither party will engage in activities that violate trade laws, anti-corruption statutes, or embargo restrictions.

Intellectual Property Rights (If Applicable): If the sales involve products embedded with intellectual property, such as patented components, copyrighted software, or trademarked branding, the contract should specify the ownership of such rights and any licensing terms or restrictions on usage.

Carriage Contract

A carriage contract is a legal agreement between a shipper (or consignor) and a carrier in which the carrier agrees, for payment, to transport goods from one location to another and deliver them to the consignee. It sets out the carrier's responsibilities for the safe handling, custody, and delivery of the goods, as well as their liability for any loss and damage during transit. The contract is usually evidenced by transport documents such as a B/L, AWB, or consignment note.

Key components of a carriage contract include:

Identification of the Contracting Parties: The primary parties typically include:

Carrier: The carrier is party responsible for performing the transportation service. Depending on the mode of transport, this may refer to a shipping line, airline, rail operator, trucking company, or a multimodal transport operator.

Consignor/shipper: The Consignor/shipper is the party who delivers the goods to the carrier for transportation. The consignor is generally responsible for initiating the shipment and ensuring that the cargo is ready for carriage in compliance with the contract's terms.

Consignee/receiver: The Consignee/receiver is the party designated to receive the goods at the final destination.

Description of Goods: An accurate and detailed description of the goods is essential for the safe handling, carriage, customs clearance, and risk management of the shipment. The description typically includes the type and nature of the goods, quantity and unit of measurement (e.g. weight, volume, or package count), packaging details, and condition of the goods at the time of shipment.

Mode of Transport: This clause identifies the method of carriage, whether the carriage is by sea, air, rail, road, or multimodal.

Route, Points of Origin, and Destination: The contract must clearly set out detailed provisions regarding the agreed route of carriage, including the points of loading, estimated time of departure, any trans-shipment arrangements, the final place of delivery, and the scheduled timeframe for completion of delivery.

Freight Charges and Payment Terms: This section provides the agreed freight rate, currency, method and time of payment, who is responsible for these payments, and carrier's lien (right to retain goods for unpaid freight).

Limitation of Liability: This clause specifies the maximum amount the carrier is liable for.

Exclusions: An exclusion clause exempts the carrier from liability for certain types of loss or damage. Typical exclusions include loss of or damage to the goods arising or resulting from act of god, act of war, inherent vice of goods, act or neglect of the shipper, and insufficiency of packing.

Notice, claim procedures, and time limits for suits: This clause governs how, when, and within what period a cargo owner can make a claim or file a lawsuit against the carrier for loss or damage. Typically, notice of loss or damage must be to notify the carrier immediately (often within three days of delivery), and all claims for loss or damage must be submitted in writing to the carrier's claims department within, usually, thirty days of delivery, accompanied by supporting documents (including survey reports, invoices, and delivery receipts), and any legal action against the carrier must be brought typically within one year after delivery or when delivery should have occurred.

Governing Law, Jurisdiction, and Dispute Resolution: This clause defines the legal framework of the agreement and the mechanism for settling disagreements. For instance, the contract may specify: 'This contract shall be governed by and construed in accordance with English law, and any dispute arising out of or in connection with it shall be referred to arbitration in London subject to the London Maritime Arbitrators Association (LMAA) Rules'.

Cargo Insurance Contract

In international trade, insurance contracts play a crucial role in managing the risks associated with the transportation and handling of goods across borders. These contracts are essential for protecting the financial interests of the parties involved from potential losses due to damage, theft, or loss of goods during transit.

A cargo insurance contract is a legal agreement between an insured party and an insurer. The insured is the party that purchases the cargo insurance.

The insurer is the insurance provider, the company that issues the cargo insurance policy. They are legally bound to provide coverage for insured risks (as per the contract) and compensate the insured party if a valid claim is made.

The beneficiary is the party entitled to receive the insurance compensation for cargo loss or damage.

Cargo insurance policies are classified into three types, namely Institute Cargo Clauses (A), (B), and (C), that is, ICC (A), (B), and (C). ICC (C) is the minimum coverage, protecting against major risks, such as fire, explosion, vessel sinking, and collision. ICC (B) provides wider coverage, including damage from earthquake and lightning. ICC (A) is known as an 'all-risks policy'. It offers the broadest coverage, including piracy, theft, and breakage. The selection of Institute Cargo Clauses (A, B, or C) should be made with reference to the nature of the goods, the specific perils associated with the chosen mode and route of transportation, and the level of protection desired by the insured party. For example, ICC (A) is preferable for fragile goods because its all-risk coverage includes protection against breakage.[3]

Certain Incoterms, namely CIF and CIP, require the exporter to provide insurance, though the required coverage level differs. Under CIF Incoterms, the seller must purchase minimum insurance coverage – ICC (C) – for the goods until they arrive at the port of destination. Under CIP Incoterms, the seller must provide higher insurance coverage – ICC (A) – until goods reach the agreed destination. The seller pays for insurance but only for the buyer's benefit. For other Incoterms, the decision to obtain insurance rests with either party and is typically based on their assessment of risk exposure and the desire to mitigate potential financial losses (International Chamber of Commerce (ICC), 2019b).

It is important to note that certain risks are not covered by default cargo insurance policies and require additional protection. For example, War and Strikes Risk Insurance covers loss due to war, terrorism, strikes, and civil unrest, which may be necessary for shipments to high-risk regions. Careful attention must also be paid to policy exclusions, which may preclude coverage for certain causes of loss such as inadequate packaging, delay-related losses, inherent vice, or wilful misconduct.

Key components of a cargo insurance contract include:

Insured Party (assured/ policyholder): The insured party is the party with an insurable interest in the goods.

Insurer: The insurer is the insurance company or underwriter that provides coverage and agrees to indemnify the insured in the event of a covered loss.

Beneficiary: The beneficiary is the person or entity entitled to receive the insurance compensation. Depending on the terms of sale, this could be the buyer, the seller, or a third party such as a bank holding shipping documents under an L/C. Under CIF and CIP Incoterms, the seller must provide cargo insurance naming the buyer as beneficiary.

Subject Matter of Insurance (Goods Insured): The contract provides a detailed description of the goods covered, specifying the type, nature, quantity, and value of the cargo. Precise identification of the insured goods is critical to determining the scope of the insurer's liability. For instance, the contract may specify: 'This policy covers ten metric tons of premium Sumatra coffee beans, clearly described and valued at USD 50,000, as detailed in Schedule A'.

Insured Value: The insured value defines the financial valuation basis for the cargo. Under CIF and CIP trade terms, the insured value is typically set at 110% of the invoice price to cover incidental expenses.

Coverage Types and Covered Risks: The scope of protection provided by the insurance contract is delineated under coverage types, which are categorised as follows:

All-risk coverage (ICC (A)): This comprehensive form of coverage indemnifies the insured against all accidental physical losses or damages to the goods, except for those specifically excluded in the policy.

Named perils coverage (ICC (B), and ICC (C)): Under this more limited form of coverage, protection is provided only for losses arising from specifically enumerated risks, such as fire, explosion, theft, and collision.

Policy Exclusions: This clause defines contract's exclusions, that is, circumstances under which the insurer bears no liability. Common exclusions include inherent vice or the intrinsic nature of the goods that causes their deterioration, improper or insufficient packaging, acts of war, strikes, riots, force majeure.

Duration of Coverage: The policy specifies where and when the coverage applies. For example, warehouse-to-warehouse coverage protects goods from the seller's premises to the buyer's designated location. Port-to-port coverage is more limited, protecting only during the sea voyage.

Premium: The premium represents the cost of the insurance coverage and is determined on the basis of several factors, including the nature and value of the goods, the mode and route of transportation, assessed risks, and type of coverage.

Claims Procedure: The contract establishes a formal procedure for submitting claims, which typically requires immediate notification upon discovery of loss or damage; submission of supporting documentation, including surveyor reports, shipping documents, commercial invoices, and photographs; and compliance with filing deadlines.

Survey and Inspection: The insurer typically reserves the right to appoint independent surveyors to investigate, document, and quantify losses or damages. The insured is obligated to facilitate such inspections and provide all relevant information necessary for accurate claim assessment.

Dispute Resolution, Governing Law, and Jurisdiction: This clause prescribes mechanisms for resolving disputes arising from policy interpretation, coverage disputes, or claim settlements. Provisions include the designation of governing law, the jurisdiction for dispute resolution, and procedures for negotiation, mediation, arbitration, or litigation.

Letter of Credit

A letter of credit (L/C) is a financial agreement issued by the buyer's bank, called the issuing bank, guaranteeing payment to the seller (exporter) for goods or services, provided that the seller meets the terms and conditions specified in the L/C.

The seller presents the required documents mutually agreed between the buyer and the seller (such as shipping documents, invoices, and insurance certificates) to the exporter's bank (called the advising bank), proving that the goods have been shipped in accordance with the L/C requirements. Once the bank confirms that the documents comply with the L/C terms, it releases payment to the seller. This ensures that the seller is paid only when the conditions specified in the L/C are met, while the buyer is assured that the goods will be delivered as per the L/C stipulations. The documents presented by the seller must strictly comply with the terms of the L/C. Any discrepancy can result in non-payment.

An L/C serves as a secure payment method for both the seller and buyer in international transactions, reducing the risk of non-payment for the seller and ensuring that the buyer pays only when documentary evidence confirms shipment per the L/C terms. The L/C is a separate contract from the sales contract, and is governed by the ICC's Uniform Customs and Practice for Documentary Credits (UCP 600). These rules set out the standard procedures for issuing and handling L/Cs in international trade and are widely accepted by banks and businesses globally.[4]

There are several types of L/Cs used in international trade, each serving different needs based on the nature of the transaction.

An *irrevocable L/C* provides greater security to the seller since the terms cannot be altered unilaterally. Once issued, it cannot be changed or cancelled without the agreement of the buyer, the seller, and the bank. A *revocable L/C*, on the contrary, can be modified or cancelled by the buyer or the issuing bank without prior consent from the seller. The revocable L/C is rarely used due to the risk it presents to the seller.

A *confirmed L/C* is an irrevocable L/C to which another bank, called the confirming bank (usually in the seller's country), adds its confirmation, guaranteeing payment even if the issuing bank fails to do so.

Usually, payment under an L/C is made immediately upon presentation of the required documents by the seller. This is often preferred by sellers because it offers prompt payment once conditions are met (payment at sight). A *usance (or deferred payment) L/C* is one in which the seller is paid after a specified period (such as 30, 60, or 90 days) following document presentation. This arrangement provides the buyer with additional time to arrange payment or generate revenue from the goods before payment is due.

A *transferable L/C* is an L/C that allows the first beneficiary (often a trader or intermediary) to transfer all or part of the L/C value to one or more second beneficiaries. These second beneficiaries are typically the actual suppliers or manufacturers of the goods, enabling the intermediary to fulfill the contract without needing their own capital to purchase the goods upfront.

A *revolving L/C* is a type of L/C that can be used for multiple transactions between the same parties over a defined period. After each payment is made, the credit limit is automatically reinstated up to the original amount, eliminating the need to establish a new L/C for each shipment.

A *standby L/C* serves as a financial guarantee rather than a payment method, providing assurance that payment will be made if the buyer defaults. Unlike commercial L/Cs that facilitate goods trade through document presentation, standby L/Cs are activated only upon non-performance and are typically used in service contracts, construction projects, lease agreements, and bid bonds where performance assurance is required.

Key components of an L/C include:

Applicant: The applicant is the buyer or importer who requests the issuing bank to open an L/C to the seller or exporter.

Beneficiary: The beneficiary is the seller or exporter who is entitled to receive payment under the L/C upon fulfilling all the specified conditions.

Issuing Bank: The issuing bank is the buyer's or importer's bank that issues an L/C and guarantees payment to the seller once the specified terms and conditions are met.

Advising Bank: The advising bank is the seller's or exporter's bank, usually located in the seller's country, that receives the L/C from the issuing bank, authenticates it, and notifies the seller of its issuance.

Amount: The amount is the maximum sum payable under the L/C, representing the issuing bank's upper limit of liability.

Terms and Conditions of Payment: This section specifies the exact requirements the seller must fulfil to receive payment. Under an L/C, payment is strictly conditional upon the beneficiary presenting fully compliant documents. Required documents typically include the commercial invoice, packing list, certificate of origin, and bill of lading.

Expiry Date: The expiry date defines the final deadline for presenting all required documents and marks the validity period of the L/C. To ensure payment, the beneficiary must submit the stipulated documents to the bank within 21 days of shipment (as required under UCP 600) and no later than the L/C expiry date.

Payment Terms: Payment terms define how and when payment will be made, providing clarity on payment timing and conditions. They are classified into two types: at sight payment and deferred payment. Under at sight payment, the issuing or nominated bank releases payment immediately upon presentation of compliant documents. A typical L/C clause would state: 'Payment under this L/C shall be made at sight upon presentation of compliant documents.' Under deferred payment, payment is made after a specified period (commonly 30, 45, 60, or 90 days) from the date of document presentation or shipment. A typical L/C clause would state: 'Payment under this L/C shall be deferred for 60 days from the date of presentation of compliant documents'.

Amendments: This clause specifies the conditions under which changes to the L/C can be made. For example, in the case of an irrevocable L/C, amendments must be agreed upon by the applicant and the beneficiary and confirmed in writing by the issuing bank.

Discrepancy Resolution: This clause explains how non-compliant document submissions are handled under the L/C in accordance with UCP 600, Article 16.

For example, a commonly used clause states: 'If discrepancies are found in the presented documents, the issuing bank shall notify the presenter no later than the close of the fifth banking day following the day of presentation. The notice will specify the discrepancies and state whether the bank is refusing the documents and holding them pending the applicant's (buyer's) waiver of the discrepancies, or returning the documents. If the applicant does not waive the discrepancies, the bank has no obligation to honour or negotiate the Letter of Credit'.

Dispute Resolution, Governing Law, and Jurisdiction: This clause establishes the legal framework governing the L/C and specifies how any disputes will be resolved. L/Cs are typically governed by the *Uniform Customs and Practice for Documentary Credits* (UPC 600) together with the domestic laws of a specified jurisdiction. The clause also defines the procedures for resolving conflicts and identifies the courts or arbitration tribunals that have authority to hear disputes arising from the L/C.

Best Practices for Using Letters of Credit

1. Understand the terms and conditions thoroughly: All terms and conditions must be clearly understood before issuing or accepting an L/C, including shipment deadlines, required documents, and the expiry date. Any discrepancy between documents and L/C terms can lead to payment delays or refusal.
2. Choose the appropriate type of L/C: The type of L/C should be selected based on the nature of the transaction, the level of risk involved, and the relationship with the trading partner. Key considerations include the need for confirmed L/C, transferability, or deferred payment terms.
3. Ensure complete and accurate documentation: One of the most critical aspects of using an L/C is ensuring that all the required documents are submitted correctly and fully comply with the L/C terms and conditions. Missing or incorrect documents can result in non-payment or delays. Double-check all details, including shipping dates, goods descriptions, quantities, invoice amounts, and party names. Even minor discrepancies can cause payment delays or rejection.
4. Work with experienced and reputable banks: Choose a bank with expertise in international trade and L/C transactions. Experienced banks can provide expert guidance on L/C terms and requirements, identify potential discrepancies early, process documents efficiently, and offer advice on risk mitigation.

Resolving International Trade Disputes

International trade contracts play a pivotal role in regulating cross-border business transactions by defining the rights and obligations of the parties involved. However, given the inherent complexity of international commerce, breaches of contract are not uncommon. They often link to either non-performance, such as the failure to deliver goods or remit payment within the timeframe stipulated in the contract, or non-conformity of goods, which occurs when the goods delivered differ in quality, quantity, or specifications from what was contractually agreed.

For a carriage contract, one of the most significant risks is the loss of or damage to cargo during transit. This may result from negligent handling, poor stowage, rough sea conditions, or theft. Incorrect or incomplete documentation – such as missing B/L, inaccurate customs declarations, or non-compliance with import/export paperwork – can lead to shipment delays or legal liability.[5]

Given the diverse sources of potential risks in international trade, governing law, jurisdiction, and dispute resolution clauses are vital components of contract design. These clauses establish the legal framework for managing conflicts by specifying the governing law that will interpret contractual terms, the jurisdiction or venue where disputes will be heard, and the mechanism for dispute resolution (negotiation, mediation, arbitration, or litigation). In the absence of well-drafted provisions, parties may face legal uncertainty, find themselves litigating in unfamiliar jurisdictions, and incur increased costs and delays in resolving disputes.

Governing Law and Jurisdiction

The governing law clause specifies the national legal system governing the contract in interpretation, validity, and enforcement of the contract. In international trade, this is crucial because parties are often from different jurisdictions with varying legal frameworks. By agreeing in advance on a governing law, the parties create legal certainty and reduce the risk of disputes over which national laws should apply. A standard formulation of this clause is 'This Agreement shall be governed by and construed in accordance with the laws of [Country], without regard to its conflict of law principles'.

The jurisdiction clause, on the other hand, determines which court or legal authority has the right to hear and determine disputes arising under the contract. Even when the governing law has been agreed, the parties must also specify the forum in which any legal proceedings will take place, whether in the courts of a particular country or through arbitration. This distinction ensures that both the applicable law (governing law) and the forum for dispute resolution (jurisdiction) are clearly defined, thereby reducing uncertainty and potential procedural conflicts.

A typical example of a jurisdiction clause is 'The courts of [Country/City] shall have exclusive jurisdiction to settle any dispute or claim arising out of or in connection with this Agreement'.

Dispute Resolution

The dispute resolution clause defines the method by which any dispute will be resolved. It may involve negotiation, mediation, arbitration, litigation, or a multi-tiered approach combining these mechanisms. Clearly specifying the chosen method in the contract helps minimise uncertainty, reduce costs, and ensure the efficient resolution of disputes.

Negotiation is the simplest and fastest method where parties try to reach a mutual agreement. It avoids legal costs and preserves business relationships. It is often applied as the first step before resorting to other mechanisms. The success, therefore, depends on the willingness to cooperate. However, it has no legally binding outcome unless formalised in a settlement agreement.

Mediation, bringing in a neutral third party (mediator), can help facilitate discussion between parties to reach a voluntary settlement. Mediation is less expensive and less time-consuming than arbitration or litigation. However, the result is non-binding unless the parties agree to formalise the outcome in a settlement agreement.

Arbitration is the most common form of dispute resolution in international trade. Arbitration is a form of alternative dispute resolution in which disputing parties agree to resolve their conflict outside of court through an independent, neutral third party (the arbitrator or arbitral tribunal). Arbitration has a number of advantages in international trade dispute resolution. First and foremost, it is private and confidential. Unlike court proceedings, arbitration is not open to the public. Confidentiality in arbitration helps preserve sensitive business information, which is often crucial in maintaining a competitive advantage. Arbitration is a neutral forum and avoids potential bias in national courts. Parties can choose arbitrators with expertise in their industry. It is faster, less expensive, and more cost-effective compared to litigation. Moreover, international arbitration awards are enforceable in over 170 countries under the New York Convention on the Recognition and Enforcement of Foreign Arbitral Awards (1958), which facilitates the enforcement of arbitration decisions globally and makes it a highly attractive option for resolving international trade disputes (UNCITRAL, 2016; Born, 2021).

Key arbitration institutions include the ICC, Swiss Arbitration Centre (SAC), London Court of International Arbitration (LCIA), and Singapore International Arbitration Centre (SIAC).[6]

The following example illustrates a multi-tier dispute resolution clause that incorporates negotiation, mediation, and arbitration, providing parties with a comprehensive mechanism for resolving disputes:

> In the event of any dispute, controversy, or claim arising out of or relating to this Agreement, including its existence, validity, interpretation, performance, or termination ('Dispute'), the Parties shall first seek to resolve the Dispute amicably through good-faith negotiations. Either Party may give written notice to the other Party describing the nature of the Dispute. The Parties shall meet (in person, by video conference, or by other agreed means) within [Days] of such notice to attempt to reach a mutually acceptable resolution.
>
> If the dispute remains unresolved within [Days], the Parties agree to submit the dispute to mediation under the rules of [Mediation Institution, e.g., ICC Mediation Rules]. The mediation shall take place in [City, Country], and the language of mediation shall be [Language].
>
> If the dispute is not resolved through mediation within [Days], the Parties agree to submit the dispute to final and binding arbitration under the rules of [Arbitration Institution, e.g., ICC, SIAC, LCIA]. The arbitration shall be conducted in [City, Country]. The number of arbitrators shall be one (or three, as agreed).[7] The language of arbitration shall be [Language]. The decision of the arbitrator(s) shall be final and binding on both parties. The arbitration award shall be enforceable under the New York Convention (1958).[8]

Litigation is the process of taking a dispute to court for resolution. In international trade, it typically involves filing a lawsuit in a court that has jurisdiction over the parties or the subject matter of the dispute. For instance, a contract may include a clause stating 'This Agreement shall be governed by and construed in accordance with the laws of [Country]. Any dispute, controversy, or claim arising out of or in connection with this Agreement, including any question regarding its existence, validity, or termination, shall be submitted to the exclusive jurisdiction of the courts of [Country]'.

Litigating international trade disputes in national courts presents numerous challenges and complications due to the cross-border nature of the transactions, differing legal systems, and enforcement difficulties. Without an agreed jurisdiction clause, parties from different countries may disagree on which national court should hear the case, with each party attempting to file in a jurisdiction favourable to their interests. For example, in a dispute between a Chinese supplier and a US buyer, each party may argue that their home country's courts should have jurisdiction.

Furthermore, fundamental differences between legal systems can affect case outcomes. Common law countries (such as the United Kingdom and Australia) rely on judicial precedent and past rulings, while civil law countries (such as France and Germany) base decisions on codified statutes. These different approaches can lead to varying interpretations of the same contractual terms and produce different legal outcomes.

International litigation is costly and time-consuming. Legal fees, expert witnesses, and translation expenses can be substantial, and cases often take many years to resolve, especially when appeals are involved. Lawyers must be licensed in the relevant jurisdiction, potentially requiring multiple legal teams across different countries. Furthermore, judgments obtained in one country are not automatically enforceable elsewhere; if the losing party holds assets abroad, additional legal proceedings are necessary to enforce the judgment and seize those assets.

In summary, the suitability of each dispute resolution method depends on the nature of the dispute, cost considerations, enforceability requirements, and the importance of preserving business relationships. Negotiation and mediation are ideal when parties prioritise relationship maintenance and cost minimisation. Arbitration is best suited for disputes requiring enforceable, confidential resolution with international recognition. Usually, litigation is employed as a last resort when other methods have failed or when parties need a binding judicial precedent.

Conclusion

This chapter has explored the essential contracts that form the backbone of international trade, namely sales contracts, carriage contracts, insurance contracts, and L/C. Each contract not only defines the mutual obligations of the parties involved but also underscores the importance of clarity and enforceability in minimising risk and ensuring transactional efficiency in complex cross-border operations. By examining these agreements and their dispute resolution mechanisms, the chapter highlighted how legal certainty serves as a critical foundation for trust, efficiency, and predictability in the global marketplace.

Yet, as vital as these contractual frameworks are to facilitating and regulating trade, the next and final chapter moves beyond the legal mechanisms of trade to ask a deeper question 'What kind of future should international trade help create'?. It explores international trade's wider role as a catalyst for positive change and examines how it can be leveraged to promote sustainability, social justice, and inclusive economic growth.

Key Takeaway

1 Multiple interrelated contracts operate simultaneously within a single international trade transaction, each serving a distinct function. For example, sales contracts define the fundamental obligations between the buyer and the seller; carriage contracts delineate the respective duties of the carrier and the shipper; cargo insurance contracts provide financial protection against loss or damage to goods during transit, binding both the insurer and the insured; and L/C facilitate secure payment by obligating the issuing bank to honour payment to the seller upon presentation of compliant documents.
2 Clear and enforceable contracts mitigate risk, reduce uncertainty, and enhance operational efficiency across global supply chains.
3 Dispute resolution mechanisms, including negotiation, mediation, arbitration, and litigation, offer structured approaches to resolving conflicts. Governing law and jurisdiction clauses establish the legal framework and venue under which these disputes will be resolved.
4 Legal certainty remains a cornerstone of international trade, fostering trust, predictability, and confidence among parties operating across diverse jurisdictions.

Notes

1 For further details on contracts for the international sale of goods, see United Nations (2010), International Institute for the Unification of Private Law (UNIDROIT) (2016), and DiMatteo et al. (2012) for a comprehensive guide to the application and interpretation of the CISG.
2 For a comprehensive discussion of the legal implications and ramifications of conducting business internationally, see Schaffer, R., Agusti, F., Dhooge, L., & Berger-Walliser, G. (2025). *International business law and its environment* (11th ed.). Cengage.
3 For further details on the Institute Cargo Clauses and marine insurance law, see Hudson and Madge (2013), and Gürses (2023). These texts provide an in-depth analysis of legal principles, interpretation, and risk coverage governing marine insurance.
4 ICC (2010). *Sets of guidance papers on recommended principles and usages around UCP 600 rules.* https://iccwbo.org/wp-content/uploads/sites/3/2023/03/Set-of-Guidance-Papers-on-Recommended-Principles-and-Usages-around-UCP600-Rules.pdf
5 For a more in-depth examination of the fundamental foundations of international trade law, see Carr and Stone (2021), Chuah (2022), and Murray et al. (2018). These works collectively offer comprehensive insights into the legal principles, regulatory frameworks, and dispute resolution mechanisms underpinning global commerce.
6 In 2023, the ICC Court registered 890 new cases. Of these, 870 were under the ICC Rules of Arbitration, and 20 were under the ICC Appointing Authority Rules (ICC, 2024); SIAC registered 663 new cases (CIARB, 2024); LCIA received 377 referrals, including 327 arbitrations pursuant to the LCIA Rules, marking a 13%

increase compared to 2022 (Pinsent Masons, 2024). SAC registered a total of 100 new cases, with 91% of these being arbitrations. The key industry sectors involved included manufacturing (9%), commodity mining and trading (11%), and banking and finance (14%). The most common types of agreements in dispute were sale of goods (33%) and services contracts (23%) (SAC, 2024).

7 The number of arbitrators shall be one or three if mutually agreed upon by the parties. In the case of three arbitrators, each party shall appoint one arbitrator, and the two appointed arbitrators shall jointly select the third, who will act as the presiding arbitrator. If a sole arbitrator is chosen, the parties shall mutually agree on the appointment. In the event the parties cannot agree on the appointment, the arbitrator(s) shall be appointed by the designated arbitral institution in accordance with its rules.

A sole arbitrator is common, especially when the dispute is relatively low in value or complexity. A single arbitrator reduces costs and speeds up the process. However, for high-value, complex, or highly sensitive disputes, it is more common to have three arbitrators to ensure a broader range of expertise and a more balanced decision-making process.

8 Further studies on the principles and practice of international commercial arbitration can be found in Born (2021) and Moses (2017). Examples of model arbitration clauses can be found at:

- International Chamber of Commerce (ICC). (n.d.-c). *Arbitration clause.* https://iccwbo.org/dispute-resolution/dispute-resolution-services/arbitration/rules-procedure/arbitration-clause/
- London Court of International Arbitration (LCIA). (n.d.). *Recommended clauses.* https://lcia.org/Dispute_Resolution_ Services/LCIA_Recommended_Clauses.aspx lcia.org
- Singapore International Arbitration Centre (SIAC). (2026). *SIAC model clause.* https://siac.org.sg/siac-model-clause

PART 5

Why Does Sustainable Trade Matter?

11

INTERNATIONAL TRADE FOR A SUSTAINABLE WORLD

Learning Objectives

1 Explore international trade as a means for promoting sustainability, social justice, and inclusive development.
2 Examine the voluntary sustainability initiatives and regulatory frameworks that support sustainable trade practices.

Trade with Purpose

Every purchase we make sends a signal through global supply chains. Can these everyday decisions contribute not only to economic growth but also to social progress and environmental protection?

Consider a consumer in Tokyo purchasing Fairtrade-certified honey from rural beekeepers in Ethiopia. This simple transaction helps ensure that small-scale producers receive fair compensation, supports community development projects such as education and healthcare, and encourages sustainable beekeeping practices that preserve local biodiversity and prevent deforestation.

Or think of a family in Paris buying a car with low CO_2 emissions that complies with stringent EU environmental standards. While meeting their mobility needs, this purchase contributes to reducing greenhouse gas emissions, stimulates innovation in green automotive technologies, and supports industries investing in cleaner production methods.

DOI: 10.4324/9781003535874-16

These choices reflect a deeper question at the core of this chapter: can international trade serve not only as a driver of economic growth but also as a catalyst for a more sustainable and inclusive world economy?

Throughout this book, we have explored the fundamental questions that shape the field of international trade: why does trade matter for us all? Why are businesses compelled to expand internationally? Why is international trade important for nations? And why do international trade laws and regulations play such a crucial role? Each chapter has unpacked the complex layers of global commerce, offering insights into the deep interconnections that define our modern world.

It is undeniable that international trade has long been celebrated as a driver of economic growth, a force that has lifted millions out of poverty and connected distant economies. Yet, in the twenty-first century, it faces increasing scrutiny, not only for what it moves across borders, but also for how it operates and at what social, economic, and environmental cost. In an era marked by climate change, inequality, and ecological degradation, the traditional paradigms of trade, efficiency, speed, and profit are no longer sufficient.

As we stand at the intersection of economic opportunity and social and planetary responsibility, this chapter pivots towards a deeper and more urgent question: what kind of future should international trade help shape? Trade should no longer be viewed purely as an economic mechanism, but as a strategic lever to advance environmental stewardship, social justice, and inclusive growth.

International Trade and Sustainability

The intersection of international trade and sustainability has become a key subject of policy and academic debate, highlighting the tensions between economic growth, environmental stewardship, and social equity.

Globalisation and trade liberalisation have enabled MNCs to shift production to countries where labour is inexpensive and regulatory protections are weak, often resulting in exploitative working conditions. The tragic collapse of the Rana Plaza factory in Bangladesh in 2013, which claimed the lives of over 1,100 garment workers, exemplifies how cost pressures in global supply chains can undermine human dignity and worker safety.[1] Environmental degradation is also another major criticism of the global trade. Trade liberalisation can incentivise the overexploitation of natural resources in countries with weak environmental governance. For example, the rapid growth of palm oil exports from Indonesia and Malaysia has been closely linked to deforestation, biodiversity loss, and the destruction of carbon-rich peatlands (Benedict & Heilmayr, 2024). Many developing countries remain locked into roles as exporters of raw materials or low-value goods, limiting their capacity to move up the value chain and leaving them vulnerable to commodity price fluctuations and external market dependency (United Nations, 2023). In addition, the expansion of trade has led to increased transportation volumes and carbon emissions, particularly through maritime shipping. Data indicated that the maritime industry accounts for around 3% of global greenhouse gas emissions (Asmussen & Ostaeyen, 2025)

The contemporary debate on international trade increasingly revolves around how it can be restructured to deliver fair, equitable, and sustainable benefits to all stakeholders, particularly developing countries and marginalised communities that have historically been disadvantaged by global economic systems. While trade has undoubtedly driven growth and innovation, without meaningful international cooperation and effective governance, trade can exacerbate inequalities, strain natural resources, and impose social and environmental costs on future generations.

There is a growing awareness and recognition that trade can be a powerful instrument for sustainable development rather than merely a vehicle for economic exchange. What began as relatively small and fragmented initiatives has, over time, evolved into more mainstream practices that embed sustainability within global trade. Many voluntary initiatives led by private actors now integrate ethical, social, and environmental principles into global supply chains. These include corporate social responsibility (CSR) programmes and certification schemes such as Fairtrade, Rainforest Alliance, and the Forest Stewardship Council, which promote responsible sourcing and improved labour and environmental practices.

In parallel, an expanding range of regulatory and legal instruments at both national and international levels has emerged, creating binding legal frameworks that compel compliance and ensure a level playing field. These include human rights and environmental due diligence laws, climate-related trade measures, and labour protection standards incorporated into bilateral and multilateral trade agreements. Together, these developments illustrate a growing realisation that trade must serve broader societal goals and align with sustainability imperatives.

This gradual but steady transformation demonstrates that international trade, when properly governed and intentionally structured, can move beyond a narrow focus on profit and efficiency. It can act as an engine of inclusive economic prosperity, environmental stewardship, and social well-being. What was once considered a niche approach has now gained momentum, signalling that sustainable trade is no longer peripheral but increasingly central to shaping the future of the global economy.

Voluntary Sustainability Initiatives in International Trade

A growing number of businesses and industries are adopting voluntary sustainability initiatives to demonstrate their commitment to ethical, social, and environmental responsibility. These initiatives are not legally mandated but increasingly function as de facto market requirements, particularly in industries where consumers, investors, and supply chain leaders demand high sustainability standards. These voluntary measures often address human rights, labour conditions, environmental impacts, fair trade practices, and corporate governance. An expanding range of voluntary sustainability initiatives is now integrated into global trade practices. Notable examples include:

Corporate social responsibility (CSR) initiatives: Many MNCs voluntarily adopt CSR frameworks to integrate sustainability into their core business strategies. These corporate efforts demonstrate that integrating sustainability into business operations can simultaneously address global challenges and enhance long-term competitiveness. For example, IKEA sources wood exclusively from Forest Stewardship Council (FSC)-certified forests,[2] promoting responsible forest management while ensuring sustainable supply chains. Starbucks implements the Coffee and Farmer Equity (CAFE) Practices programme[3] to guarantee ethical sourcing, sustainable farming, and protection of workers' rights across its coffee supply chain. Google has committed to carbon neutrality since 2007 and aims to operate entirely on carbon-free energy by 2030. Lego strives to transition all its products and packaging to sustainable materials by 2030. Salesforce applies a 1–1–1 philanthropic model, dedicating 1% of its equity, products, and employee time to social and community development efforts worldwide. Nike emphasises diversity, equity, and inclusion. Apple is pursuing comprehensive sustainability goals, including achieving carbon neutrality across its products and entire supply chain by 2030, emphasising renewable energy and resource efficiency.[4]

Fairtrade certification: Fairtrade standards aim to improve livelihoods of small-scale producers in developing countries by guaranteeing fair prices, promoting safe working conditions, providing community development premiums, and supporting sustainable production practices. This certification helps marginalised producers integrate into global markets under more equitable terms.[5] Examples of Fairtrade-certified products widely available in global retail stores – such as Whole Foods Market, Tesco, Sainsbury's, and Walmart – include Equal Exchange Fairtrade-certified coffee, Divine Chocolate Fairtrade-certified chocolate, GloryBee Fairtrade-certified organic honey, and La Riojana Fairtrade-certified wine.

Rainforest Alliance certification: Rainforest Alliance certification emphasises four core pillars: biodiversity conservation, improved livelihoods and human rights, climate resilience, and sustainable land management. Certified producers are required to implement practices that minimise environmental harm, ensure fair treatment and safe working conditions, and promote community development. The certification process involves regular auditing and compliance with the Rainforest Alliance Sustainable Agriculture Standard, which is periodically updated to reflect evolving best practices and stakeholder input. This certification plays a critical role in GVCs, particularly for commodities such as coffee, cocoa, tea, and bananas.[6]

Environmental Management Systems (ISO 14001): Developed by the International Organization for Standardization (ISO), ISO 14001 provides a globally recognised framework for organisations to manage and reduce their environmental footprint. It offers a framework for organisations to systematically manage environmental risks, improve resource efficiency, and demonstrate compliance with environmental regulations. Adoption of ISO 14001 allows firms to improve resource efficiency, minimise waste, ensure regulatory compliance, and demonstrate environmental stewardship to international stakeholders.[7]

Social Accountability Standard (SA8000): Administered by Social Accountability International (SAI), SA8000 focuses on protecting workers' rights across global supply chains. The standard addresses core labour issues, including child labour, forced labour, health and safety, discrimination, working hours, freedom of association, and fair compensation, aligning with internationally recognised labour conventions.[8]

FSC certification: FSC certification promotes responsible forest management that balances environmental conservation, social equity, and economic viability. FSC certification assures buyers that timber and forest products originate from sustainably managed forests, contributing to biodiversity protection and the rights of indigenous communities.[9]

Environmental, social, and governance (ESG) reporting: ESG frameworks encourage businesses to disclose their performance across the ESG dimensions. While often voluntary, ESG reporting increasingly influences investor decisions, strengthens corporate accountability, and enhances reputation, particularly as global financial markets integrate sustainability criteria into investment analyses.[10]

Eco-labels and product certification schemes: Eco-labels such as the EU Ecolabel serve as voluntary labels promoting environmental excellence for products and services meeting high ecological standards throughout their lifecycle.[11] *Energy Star* is a US Government-backed symbol for energy efficiency, helping consumers and businesses save money while protecting the environment.[12] *Marine Stewardship Council* (MSC) is an international non-profit organisation that certifies sustainable fishing practices to ensure healthy oceans and seafood traceability.[13] *Organic Certifications*, such as IFOAM (International Federation of Organic Agriculture Movements) standards, a set of standards ensuring agricultural products are grown and processed using natural substances and sustainable practices.[14] These labels guide consumer choices towards social and environmentally responsible products and create competitive incentives for producers to adopt sustainable practices.

The Adoption of Voluntary Sustainability Initiatives in International Trade

The adoption of voluntary sustainability measures in international trade extends across a diverse range of actors, reflecting the growing recognition that responsible business practices are not only ethically desirable but increasingly necessary for market access and long-term competitiveness.

MNCs are among the leading adopters, as they face significant pressure from consumers, investors, and civil society to demonstrate environmental and social responsibility across complex global supply chains. Global retailers and supply chain leaders also play a critical role in driving adoption. They often require suppliers to comply with specific voluntary standards as a condition for maintaining business relationships. Exporters increasingly adopt voluntary standards to secure access to high-value international markets.

Financial institutions and global investors are integrating ESG frameworks into their investment criteria, encouraging firms to adopt these standards as part of broader corporate risk management and reputation-building strategies. Financial institutions such as BlackRock have incorporated ESG screening into lending and investment decisions.[15] In addition, public procurement agencies in several countries also incentivise adoption by incorporating voluntary standards into government purchasing requirements. For instance, many EU member states give preference to suppliers who comply with eco-labels, ISO 14001, and social accountability standards as part of sustainable public procurement policies.[16]

Non-governmental organisations (NGOs), industry associations, and certification bodies play an essential supporting role by developing standards, providing training, conducting audits, and monitoring compliance, thereby strengthening the credibility and global recognition of voluntary sustainability measures.

Last but not least, ethical consumerism has become a powerful market driver for voluntary sustainability initiatives in international trade. Increasingly, consumers actively seek products that reflect ethical sourcing, fair labour standards, and environmentally responsible production. These market-based pressures incentivise both producers and global brands to exceed minimum legal standards and adopt sustainability as a core business strategy.

Collectively, these voluntary measures complement legal and regulatory efforts by fostering a culture of corporate responsibility, enhancing consumer awareness, and promoting sustainable practices across international supply chains. While voluntary, these standards are increasingly becoming de facto requirements for access to global markets, especially among MNCs, retailers, and financial institutions committed to sustainable procurement and investment practices.

Regulatory and Legal Instruments for Sustainability in International Trade

While voluntary initiatives play a crucial role in encouraging firms to adopt socially and environmentally responsible business practices, the growing complexity of global trade and international supply chains and the urgent need for enforceable environmental and social outcomes have led governments and international organisations to establish legally binding instruments that integrate sustainability directly into the rules governing international trade. These legal instruments ensure that businesses align their activities with legally mandated standards on human rights, environmental protection, and ethical conduct, or face penalties such as fines or import bans. Notable examples include:

Carbon pricing and border adjustment mechanisms: One of the most prominent legal tools used to internalise the environmental costs of production is carbon pricing. Mechanisms such as carbon taxes and emissions trading systems (ETS) directly impose costs on carbon emissions, incentivising firms to adopt cleaner production methods (World Bank, 2023). The European Union's Emissions Trading Scheme (EU ETS), for example, caps total emissions from energy-intensive sectors and allows companies to trade emission allowances within this cap, thus using market forces to drive emission reductions (European Commission, 2021). Sweden, for example, has implemented one of the world's highest carbon taxes, exceeding $100 per ton of CO_2, which has significantly reduced emissions while maintaining economic competitiveness (OECD, 2021).

Complementing these measures, the European Union has introduced the Carbon Border Adjustment Mechanism (CBAM) as part of its Green Deal strategy.[17] CBAM imposes tariffs on certain imported goods, such as cement, iron and steel, and aluminum, corresponding to their embedded carbon emissions. This measure serves two primary purposes: first, it ensures foreign producers are held to environmental standards comparable to those of domestic firms; and second, it mitigates the risk of carbon leakage, where companies in a country with strict climate policies move their carbon-intensive production to other countries with looser environmental regulations, leading to no net reduction in global emissions.

Supply chain due diligence laws: Several jurisdictions have moved towards legally binding mandatory human rights and environmental due diligence requirements, obligating firms to actively assess, monitor, and mitigate environmental and human rights risks throughout their global supply chains. The European Union is currently finalising its Corporate Sustainability Due Diligence Directive (CSDDD),[18] while some national legislations – such as Germany's Supply Chain Due Diligence Act (2021)[19] and France's Duty of Vigilance Law (2017)[20] – have already established comprehensive obligations for MNEs (European Commission, n.d.-e).

Trade restrictions on unsustainable practices: International trade law increasingly incorporates bans on products linked to illegal or unsustainable practices. For instance, the European Union's Illegal, Unreported, and Unregulated (IUU) Fishing Regulation prevents seafood derived from illegal fishing activities from entering the EU market, contributing to the sustainability of global fisheries (European Council, 2024). Similarly, the recently adopted EU Deforestation Regulation (EUDR) prohibits imports of commodities such as soy, coffee, cocoa, palm oil, and timber if they are linked to deforestation or forest degradation. Importers must demonstrate that these goods do not contribute to global deforestation through strict due diligence requirements (European Commission, n.d.-i).

International environmental agreements: At the multilateral level, several legal frameworks directly regulate trade to protect biodiversity and endangered species. The Convention on International Trade in Endangered Species of Wild Fauna and Flora (CITES) regulates international trade in wildlife products to prevent threats to endangered species. CITES legally binds its 184 member countries to control trade through a permit system applied to approximately 36,000 species listed across three Appendices to ensure that the international movement of specimens is legal and traceable. Appendix I lists species most threatened with extinction (e.g., tigers); commercial trade is generally prohibited. Appendix II lists species that may become threatened; trade is permitted but requires permits to ensure it is sustainable (e.g., most corals). Appendix III lists species that a single country has asked other Parties to help control trade in (e.g., certain populations of walrus) (CITES, 2023).

Circular economy and product stewardship regulations: In addition to controlling trade in raw materials, many legal mandates promote circular economy principles through product stewardship obligations. The European Union's Waste Electrical and Electronic Equipment (WEEE) directive requires producers to manage the collection, recycling, and safe disposal of electronic waste, while the Ecodesign Directive sets energy efficiency and environmental performance standards for products sold in EU markets (European Commission, 2022, n.d.-f). This framework aims to improve products across their entire life cycle, ensuring they are more durable, repairable, and resource-efficient. It moves beyond energy alone, covering a broad range of physical goods from electronics and appliances to other sectors such as textiles and furniture, making sustainable products the norm.

Labour and human rights trade measures: Several jurisdictions have tied trade access to compliance with labour and human rights standards. For example, the US Uyghur Forced Labor Prevention Act (UFLPA) prohibits the importation of goods that are mined, produced, or manufactured wholly or in part in China's Xinjiang Uyghur Autonomous Region, unless the importer can provide clear and convincing evidence that the goods were not produced with forced labour (US Customs and Border Protection, 2023). Moreover, many modern FTAs incorporate enforceable Trade and Sustainable Development (TSD) Chapters that require parties to uphold labour rights, environmental protections, and sustainable development objectives as conditions for preferential market access. For instance, the

European Union–Vietnam Free Trade Agreement (EVFTA) contains a dedicated TSD chapter that commits both parties to implement core International Labour Organization (ILO) conventions, promote sustainable forestry and fisheries management, and uphold the Paris Agreement on climate change.[21]

Taken together, these legal mandates reflect a global shift towards embedding sustainability directly into the legal architecture of international trade. While voluntary initiatives remain important, legally binding regulations are increasingly setting minimum standards that companies must meet to access key global markets.

Conclusion

International trade has long been a powerful driver of economic growth, technological progress, and innovation, fostering deeper connections and collaborations among nations. Yet its impact ultimately depends on how it is managed and governed. When driven solely by short-term profit and pursued without regard for people or the planet, trade can unintentionally widen inequalities and deplete natural resources.

Today, there is growing global demand that trade must serve a higher purpose beyond the simple exchange of goods and services. This shift is reflected in two complementary pillars that are reshaping the future of trade. On one side, voluntary initiatives – such as corporate social responsibility, sustainability standards, and ethical supply chain practices – demonstrate how businesses and consumers can actively drive positive change. On the other hand, regulatory and legal frameworks create a foundation of enforceable rules, ensuring that all actors meet minimum sustainability standards. By integrating both voluntary efforts and legally binding frameworks, international trade is being reoriented, guided, and directed to actively advance global economic, social, and environmental sustainability.

I would like to conclude this book with my deepest conviction that international trade, when properly governed and responsibly managed, can serve as a powerful instrument for meaningful development, not only in economic terms, but also in ways that promote social justice, protect our environment, and improve the quality of life for all.

The late Dr Puey Ungphakorn's speech, 'The Quality of Life of a Southeast Asian', widely known as 'From Womb to Tomb', invites deep reflection on what truly constitutes a meaningful quality of life from the day we are born to the day we die, and what development should genuinely aspire to achieve. True development is not merely about material wealth; it is people-centred, ensuring dignity, equality, and well-being for every individual through equitable access to comprehensive healthcare, education, meaningful work, and social participation within a fair, just, and sustainable society. As he expressed:[22]

> *'I would like my country to get a fair price for the products that I and my fellow citizens create.*
>
> *As a farmer, I would like to have my own plot of land, with a system which gives me access to credit, to new agricultural technology and to markets, and a fair price for my produce.*
>
> *As a worker, I would want to have some share, some sense of participation in the factory in which I work.'*

Ultimately, building a sustainable global trade requires more than government regulation and corporate responsibility. Individuals – whether as consumers, business leaders, policymakers, or global citizens – also possess the agency to transform a trade system that may cause exploitation into one that fosters fair trade, ethical business practices, and environmental stewardship.Through this collective endeavour, we can ensure that international trade serves the broader interests of humanity and the planet, not just today but for generations to come.

Key Takeaway

1. International trade holds the potential to become a force for positive global change. This transformation is anchored in two complementary pillars – voluntary sustainability initiatives by businesses and civil society, and robust regulatory and legal frameworks established by governments.
2. Building sustainable global trade requires collective action at all levels – from informed consumer choices and responsible business conduct to sound policymaking that fosters economic growth with fairness, equity, and environmental stewardship for current and future generations.

Notes

1. For further information on the Rana Plaza disaster and its aftermath, see International Labour Organization (n.d.); Paton (2023); Holland (2023); Friedman (2023); Hunt (2023).
2. The FSC is an international non-profit organization that sets standards for responsible forest management and provides certification for sustainably sourced wood and paper products. Further details can be found at Forest Stewardship Council. (n.d.). *What is FSC certification?* https://fsc.org/en/label
3. The CAFE Practices programme is Starbucks' ethical sourcing verification system, developed in partnership with Conservation International, focusing on product quality, social responsibility, environmental leadership, and economic transparency.

Further details can be found at Starbucks. (n.d.). *C.A.F.E. practices ethical sourcing program*. https://www.starbucks.com/responsibility/sourcing/coffee

4 Further details and examples of CSR initiatives can be found at:
 - Goodera. (May 2, 2025). *12 Inspiring corporate social responsibility examples from brands in action*. https://www.goodera.com/blog/corporate-social-responsibility-examples
 - Harvard Business School Online. (2019, June 6). *6 Examples of corporate social responsibility that were successful*. https://online.hbs.edu/blog/post/corporate-social-responsibility-examples

5 Further information is available from Fairtrade International: https://www.fairtrade.net

6 Further information can be found on the official Rainforest Alliance website: https://www.rainforest-alliance.org

7 Additional information about the ISO 14000 family of standards is available at the official ISO website: https://www.iso.org/standards/popular/iso-14000-family

8 Additional information about the SA8000 standard can be found on the official Social Accountability International website: https://sa-intl.org/programs/sa8000/

9 Additional information about FSC certification is available on the official FSC website: https://fsc.org/en

10 Additional information about ESG reporting is available on the PwC website: https://www.pwc.com/sk/en/environmental-social-and-corporate-governance-esg/esg-reporting.html

11 More information is available at the official EU Ecolabel website: https://environment.ec.europa.eu/topics/circular-economy/eu-ecolabel_en

12 Additional information can be found at the official Energy Star website: https://www.energystar.gov

13 Further details are available at the MSC website: https://www.msc.org

14 More information is available from the International Federation of Organic Agriculture Movements (IFOAM). https://www.ifoam.bio and IFOAM (2020).

15 Further details are available at *Our fiduciary approach to sustainability and the low-carbon transition*. https://www.blackrock.com/corporate/insights/our-approach-to-sustainability

16 For example, see European Commission. (2024). *Green Public Procurement: Procuring goods, services and works with a reduced environmental impact throughout their life cycle*. https://green-forum.ec.europa.eu/green-business/green-public-procurement_en, and *Green public procurement criteria and requirements*. https://green-forum.ec.europa.eu/green-business/green-public-procurement/gpp-criteria-and-requirements_en

17 The EU Green Deal is the European Union's overarching strategy to transform its economy into a sustainable, climate-neutral, and resource-efficient system by 2050. Key pillars of the EU Green Deal include:

Climate Action & Energy Transition, aiming to cut greenhouse gas emissions by 55% by 2030 (compared to 1990 levels), phase out fossil fuels and rapidly expand renewable energy sources, improve energy efficiency and promote a circular economy model.

Sustainable Industry & Trade, aiming to support clean technologies and green innovation in EU industries, introduce a CBAM to prevent carbon leakage (companies relocating production to countries with weaker climate rules), and align trade policy with sustainability goals, including integration of green clauses in trade agreements.

Biodiversity & Agriculture, aiming to protect ecosystems, forests, and oceans, and promote sustainable farming under the Farm to Fork Strategy, reducing the use of pesticides and fertilisers.

Circular Economy, aiming to design products for reuse, repair, and recycling, reduce waste and set stricter standards for packaging, textiles, and electronics. Further information can be accessed at European Commission. (n.d.-k). *The European Green Deal: Striving to be the first climate-neutral continent.* https://commission.europa.eu/strategy-and-policy/priorities-2019-2024/european-green-deal_en

18 The CSDDD is a proposed EU directive that will require large companies operating in the European Union to identify, prevent, and mitigate adverse human rights and environmental impacts throughout their global value chains. Further details can be accessed on European Commission. (n.d.-e). *Corporate sustainability due diligence.* Retrieved February 20, 2025, from https://commission.europa.eu/business-economy-euro/doing-business-eu/sustainability-due-diligence-responsible-business/corporate-sustainability-due-diligence_en

19 Germany's Supply Chain Due Diligence Act (2021) is national legislation requiring German companies with more than 3,000 employees (and, from 2024 onward, those with more than 1,000 employees) to conduct risk assessments and implement measures to address human rights and environmental risks in their supply chains. Further details can be accessed in Federal Ministry of Labour and Social Affairs. (n.d.). *Act on corporate due diligence obligations in supply chains.* Retrieved February 20, 2025, from https://www.bmas.de/EN/Europe-and-the-World/International/Supply-Chain-Act/supply-chain-act.html

20 France's Duty of Vigilance Law (2017) requires large French companies employing more than 5,000 employees in France, or more than 10,000 employees worldwide (including subsidiaries), to establish and implement a vigilance plan. This plan must identify and prevent serious violations of human rights, fundamental freedoms, health and safety risks, and environmental damage arising from their own activities, those of their subsidiaries, and their suppliers or subcontractors. Further details can be accessed in French Ministry for Europe and Foreign Affairs. (2017). *New law on the duty of vigilance of parent companies and on its affiliated entities.* Retrieved February 20, 2025, from https://www.diplomatie.gouv.fr/IMG/pdf/law_on_the_duty_of_vigilance_cle8b1211.pdf, and Business & Human Rights Resource Centre. (n.d.). *France's duty of vigilance law.* Retrieved February 20, 2025, from https://www.business-humanrights.org/en/big-issues/corporate-legal-accountability/frances-duty-of-vigilance-law/

21 European Union. (n.d.). *EU-Vietnam trade agreement. Standards and values.* Retrieved February 20, 2025, from https://circabc.europa.eu/ui/group/09242a36-a438-40fd-a7af-fe32e36cbd0e/library/d9bcaa49-3b0d-4da0-9294-f227159b8c16/details

22 Additional information on Dr. Puey Ungphakorn, along with the full text of his essay *'The Quality of Life of a Southeast Asian'*, is available at the following links: https://www.nectec.or.th/users/htk/dr-puey/index.html and https://www.nectec.or.th/users/htk/dr-puey/womb-tomb.html

BIBLIOGRAPHY

Abu Dhabi Customs. (n.d.). *Restricted and prohibited goods.* Retrieved July 21, 2025, from https://www.adcustoms.gov.ae/en/Restricted-Banned-Commodities

ACERIS Law LLC. (2020). *Incoterms in international trade.* https://www.acerislaw.com/incoterms-in-international-trade

African Union. (n.d.-a). *East African community (EAC).* https://au.int/en/recs/eac

African Union. (n.d.-b). *Economic community of West African States (ECOWAS).* https://au.int/en/recs/ecowas

African Union. (n.d.-c). *The African Union in a nutshell.* https://au.int/en/au-nutshell

Air Cargo News. (2024, September 2). *Top 25 cargo carriers: Cargo goes slow on growth in 2023.* https://www.aircargonews.net/top-25-cargo-carriers-cargo-goes-slow-on-growth-in-2023/1073135.article

AirAsia. (n.d.). *About AirAsia.* https://newsroom.airasia.com/about-us/#gsc.tab=0

Al Jazeera. (2025, April 28). *Power outage hits Spain and Portugal: What happened and what was affected.* https://www.aljazeera.com/news/2025/4/28/power-outage-hits-spain-and-portugal-what-happened-and-what-was-affected

Alphaliner. (2025). *Top 100 carriers.* https://alphaliner.axsmarine.com/PublicTop100/

American Chamber of Commerce. (n.d.). *About AmCham network.* https://www.uschamber.com/

Andrews, J. (1999). *Peppers: The domesticated capsicums.* University of Texas Press.

AP. (2024, December 6). *The EU and a South American trade bloc reach a giant trade deal after 25 years of talks.* https://apnews.com/article/44ca8d0eef524b84014ad266c286f8fe

Asia-Pacific Economic Cooperation (APEC). (2022). *Study on tariffs: Analysis of the RCEP tariff liberalization schedules.* https://research.apec.org/rcep/files/Study%20on%20tariffs_RCEP%20(Final)%2006May2022.pdf

Asia-Pacific Economic Cooperation (APEC). (2024). *About APEC.* https://www.apec.org/about-us/about-apec

Asian Development Bank. (n.d.). *What we do.* https://www.adb.org/what-we-do

Asmussen, M., & Van Ostaeyen, P. (2025, May 2). How real-time emissions tracking can help decarbonize the maritime industry. *World Economic Forum.*

Retrieved July 20, 2025, from https://www.weforum.org/stories/2025/05/decarbonize-maritime-industry-real-time-emissions-tracking/
Association of German Chambers of Industry and Commerce (DIHK). (n.d.). *The AHK network – German Chambers Abroad.* https://www.dihk.de/en
Association of Southeast Asian Nations (ASEAN). (n.d.-a). *Free trade agreements with dialogue partners.* Association of Southeast Asian Nations. https://asean.org/free-trade-agreements-with-dialogue-partners/
Association of Southeast Asian Nations (ASEAN). (n.d.-b). *Overview: About ASEAN.* https://asean.org/about-asean/
Balassa, B. (1961). *The theory of economic integration.* R. D. Irwin.
BBC News. (2011, November 1). *Hard disk and camera makers hit by Thai floods.* https://www.bbc.com/news/technology-15534614
BBC News. (2021, March 29). *The cost of the Suez Canal blockage.* https://www.bbc.com/news/business-56559073
BBC News. (2022, September 27). *iPhone in India: Apple makes new handset in India in shift from China.* https://www.bbc.com/news/business-63043083
BBC News. (2024a, April 30). *Tensions grow as China ramps up global mining for Green Tech.* https://www.bbc.com/news/world-68896707
BBC News. (2024b, September 24). *CrowdStrike: What was the impact of the global IT outage.* https://www.bbc.com/news/articles/cr54m92ermgo
BBC News. (2025, April 28). *Live: Spain and Portugal hit by major power outage.* https://www.bbc.com/news/live/c9wpq8xrvd9t?page=2
Benedict, J., & Heilmayr, R. (2024). Indonesian palm oil exports and deforestation. *Trase.* https://doi.org/10.48650/0ZP9-GH11
Bernstein, W. J. (2008). *A splendid exchange: How trade shaped the world.* Grove Press.
Bhagwati, J. (2004). *In defense of globalization.* Oxford University Press.
BlackRock. (n.d.). *Our fiduciary approach to sustainability and the low-carbon transition.* Retrieved July 28, 2025, from https://www.blackrock.com/corporate/insights/our-approach-to-sustainability
Bloom, J. M. (2001). *Paper before print: The history and impact of paper in the Islamic world.* Yale University Press.
BMW Group. (2023). *Annual report 2022.* https://www.bmwgroup.com/en/investor-relations/company-reports.html
Born, G. B. (2021). *International commercial arbitration* (3rd ed.). Kluwer Law International.
Boston Consulting Group & Semiconductor Industry Association. (2021). *Strengthening the global semiconductor value chain.* https://www.semiconductors.org/wp-content/uploads/2021/05/BCG-x-SIA-Strengthening-the-Global-Semiconductor-Value-Chain-April-2021_1.pdf
Bown, C. P. (2021). *The US-China trade war and phase one agreement.* The Peterson Institute for International Economics. https://www.piie.com/sites/default/files/documents/wp21-2.pdf
Brander, J. A., & Spencer, B. J. (1985). Export subsidies and international market share rivalry. *Journal of International Economics, 18*(1–2), 83–100.
Business & Human Rights Resource Centre. (n.d.). *France's Duty of Vigilance Law.* Retrieved February 20, 2025, from https://www.business-humanrights.org/en/big-issues/corporate-legal-accountability/frances-duty-of-vigilance-law/
Capela, J. J. (2015). *Import/export kit for dummies* (3rd ed.). Wiley.
Caribbean Community and Common Market (CARICOM). (n.d.-a). *Objectives of CARICOM and functional cooperation.* Retrieved June 25, 2025, from https://caricom.org/what-we-do
Caribbean Community and Common Market (CARICOM). (n.d.-b). *Member states, associate members, and observers.* Retrieved June 25, 2025, from https://caricom.org/member-states/

Carr, I., & Stone, P. (2021). *International trade law* (8th ed.). Routledge.

Cavusgil, S. T., Knight, G., & Riesenberger, J. R. (2021). *International business: The new realities* (5th ed.). Pearson.

Chartered Institute of Arbitrators. (2024, October 10). *Numbers don't lie: International commercial arbitration statistics 2023.* Retrieved July 28, 2025, from https://www.ciarb.org/news-listing/numbers-don-t-lie-international-commercial-arbitration-statistics-2023/ciarb.org

Chen, Y., Fang, J., & Liu, D. (2023). The effects of Trump's trade war on US financial markets. *Journal of International Money and Finance.* https://doi.org/10.1016/j.jimonfin.2023.102842

China International Commercial Court. (n.d.). *A brief introduction of China International Commercial Court.* https://cicc.court.gov.cn/html/1/219/193/195/index.html

Chuah, J. (2022). *Law of international trade* (7th ed.). Routledge.

Chughtai, A., & Haddad, M. (2025, April 9). Eight charts that reveal the economic impact of Trump's tariffs. *Al Jazeera.* https://www.aljazeera.com/economy/2025/4/9/eight-charts-that-reveal-the-economic-impact-of-trumps-tariffs

CITES. (2023). *What is CITES? Convention on international trade in endangered species of Wild Fauna and Flora.* https://cites.org/eng/disc/what.php

CNBC. (2025, March 25). *Chinese EV giant BYD outpaces Tesla with annual sales of more than $100 billion.* https://www.cnbc.com/2025/03/25/ev-giant-byd-outpaces-tesla-with-annual-sales-of-over-100-billion.html?msockid=3a1398039907628d3aad8df098676312

CNN Business. (2024, July 24). *We finally know what caused the global tech outage – and how much it cost.* https://edition.cnn.com/2024/07/24/tech/crowdstrike-outage-cost-cause/index.html

Coca-Cola Company. (2023). *2022 Annual report.* https://investors.coca-colacompany.com/

Cohen, S. (n.d.). *The route to Japan's voluntary export restraints on automobiles.* Retrieved July 27, 2025, from https://nsarchive2.gwu.edu/japan/scohenwp.htm

Commission Nationale de l'Informatique et des Libertés (CNIL). (2019, January 21). *The CNIL's restricted committee imposes a financial penalty of 50 Million euros against GOOGLE LLC.* https://www.edpb.europa.eu/news/national-news/2019/cnils-restricted-committee-imposes-financial-penalty-50-million-euros_en

Comunidad Andina. (n.d.-a). *Qué es la Comunidad Andina.* Retrieved June 25, 2025, from https://www.comunidadandina.org/quienes-somos/

Comunidad Andina. (n.d.-b). *Países miembros.* Retrieved June 25, 2025, from https://www.comunidadandina.org/quienes-somos/paises-miembros/

Comunidad Andina. (n.d.-c). *Cronología/Sistema Andino de Integración.* Retrieved June 25, 2025, from https://www.comunidadandina.org/quienes somos/cronologia/

Council for the Development of Cambodia. (n.d.). *Textile and apparel.* Retrieved July 17, 2025, from https://cdc.gov.kh/home/textile-and-aparel/

Council on Foreign Relations. (2025, April 23). *The U.S. trade deficit: How much does it matter?* Council on Foreign Relations. https://www.cfr.org/backgrounder/us-trade-deficit-how-much-does-it-matter

Daly, M. (2024, May 15). New US tariffs on Chinese electric vehicles, batteries and solar cells could raise consumer prices. *AP News.* Retrieved July 27, 2025, from https://www.theguardian.com/world/article/2024/aug/26/canada-tariff-china-electric-vehicles

Daniels, J. D., Radebaugh, L. H., & Sullivan, D. P. (2021). *International business: Environments and operations* (17th ed.). Pearson.

Davis, S. J. (2019). *Rising policy uncertainty.* National Bureau of Economic Research Working Paper No. 26243. https://www.nber.org/papers/w26243

De Mente, B. L. (2014). *Japan's cultural code words: 233 Key terms that explain the attitudes and behavior of the Japanese*. Tuttle Publishing.
Department of Islamic Development Malaysia (JAKIM). (2014). *Manual procedure for Malaysia Halal certification (Third revision) 2014*. https://irp.cdn-website.com/18f14595/files/uploaded/MPPHM2014BI.pdf#:~:text=1.1%20This%20Manual%20Procedure%20for%20Malaysia%20Halal%20Certification,complied%20with%2C%20in%20managing%20the%20Malaysia%20Halal%20Certification
Deutsche Welle. (2024, January 10). *Indian companies struggle to stop ransomware attacks*.https://www.dw.com/en/indian-companies-struggle-to-stop-ransomware-attacks/a-70374977
DHL Global Forwarding. (n.d.). *Incoterms® explained: Let us help you make the most of Incoterms® 2020*. https://www.dhl.com/th-en/home/global-forwarding/freight-forwarding-education-center/incoterms-explained.html#:~:text=Incoterms%C2%AE%20meaning%3A%20With%20Free,the%20shipment%20for%20export%20customs.
DiMatteo, L. A., Dhooge, L. J., Greene, S., Maurer, V., & Pagnattaro, M. (2012). *International sales law: A guide to the CISG*. Cambridge University Press.
East African Community Secretariat. (2023). *Overview of EAC*. https://www.eac.int/overview-of-eac
Edward, S. (2024, April 9). *Behind the Toyota supply chain*. https://www.thomasnet.com/insights/behind-the-toyota-supply-chain/
Euronews. (2025, April 28). *Spain, Portugal and parts of France hit by massive power outage*. https://www.euronews.com/my-europe/2025/04/28/spain-portugal-and-parts-of-france-hit-by-massive-power-outage
European Central Bank. (n.d.). *Overview of the Euro?* Retrieved June 25, 2025, from https://www.ecb.europa.eu/euro/html/index.en.html
European Commission. (2019, November 21). *Final green light to the EU-Singapore Free Trade Agreement – Council of the European Union approves EUSFTA*. Press Release. https://www.consilium.europa.eu/en/press/press-releases/2019/11/08/final-green-light-to-the-eu-singapore-free-trade-agreement/
European Commission. (2021). *EU emissions trading system (EU ETS)*. https://ec.europa.eu/clima/eu-action/eu-emissions-trading-system-eu-ets_en
European Commission. (2022). *Circular economy action plan*. https://ec.europa.eu/environment/strategy/circular-economy-action-plan_en
European Commission. (n.d.-a). *The EU in brief*. Retrieved June 25, 2025, from https://european-union.europa.eu/principles-countries-history_en
European Commission. (n.d.-b). *Trade in plants & plant products from non-EU countries*. https://food.ec.europa.eu/plants/plant-health-and-biosecurity/trade-plants-plant-products-non-eu-countries_en
European Commission. (n.d.-c). *Andean community*. Retrieved June 25, 2025, from https://policy.trade.ec.europa.eu/eu-trade-relationships-country-and-region/countries-and-regions/andean-community_en
European Commission. (n.d.-d). *Corporate sustainability due diligence*. https://commission.europa.eu/business-economy-euro/doing-business-eu/sustainability-due-diligence-responsible-business/corporate-sustainability-due-diligence_en#:~:text=On%2025%20July%202024%2C%20the%20Directive%20on%20corporate,companies%E2%80%99%20operations%20and%20across%20their%20global%20value%20chains.
European Commission. (n.d.-e). *Corporate sustainability due diligence*. Retrieved February 20, 2025, from https://commission.europa.eu/business-economy-euro/doing-business-eu/sustainability-due-diligence-responsible-business/corporate-sustainability-due-diligence_en
European Commission. (n.d.-f). *EU ecolabel*. Retrieved July 28, 2025, from https://environment.ec.europa.eu/topics/circular-economy/eu-ecolabel_en

European Commission. (n.d.-g). *EU-Mercosur agreement.* Retrieved June 25, 2025, from https://policy.trade.ec.europa.eu/eu-trade-relationships-country-and-region/countries-and-regions/mercosur/eu-mercosur-agreement_en

European Commission. (n.d.-h). *Hormones in meat.* European Commission – Food Safety. Retrieved July 21, 2025, from https://food.ec.europa.eu/food-safety/chemical-safety/hormones-meat_en

European Commission. (n.d.-i). *Regulation on deforestation-free products.* https://environment.ec.europa.eu/topics/forests/deforestation/regulation-deforestation-free-products_en

European Commission. (n.d.-j). *Sanctions adopted following Russia's military aggression against Ukraine.* Retrieved July 23, 2025, from https://finance.ec.europa.eu/eu-and-world/sanctions-restrictive-measures/sanctions-adopted-following-russias-military-aggression-against-ukraine_en

European Commission. (n.d.-k). *The European green deal.* European Commission. Retrieved July 28, 2025, from https://commission.europa.eu/strategy-and-policy/priorities-2019–2024/european-green-deal_en

European Commission. (n.d.-l). *Principles, countries, history.* Retrieved June 25, 2025, from https://european-union.europa.eu/principles-countries-history_en

European Commission. (n.d.-m). *Countries using the Euro.* Retrieved June 25, 2025, from https://european-union.europa.eu/institutions-law-budget/euro/countries-using-euro_en

European Council. (2024). *Questions and answers on illegal, unreported and unregulated (IUU) fishing.* https://ec.europa.eu/commission/presscorner/detail/pt/qanda_24_2882

European Data Protection Board (EDPB). (2020, July 14). *Belgian DPA imposes 600,000 fine on Google Belgium for not respecting the right to be forgotten.* https://www.edpb.europa.eu/news/national-news/2020/belgian-dpa-imposes-eu600000-fine-google-belgium-not-respecting-right-be_en

European Data Protection Board (EDPB). (2023, May 22). *1.2 Billion euro fine for Facebook as a result of EDPB binding decision.* https://www.edpb.europa.eu/news/news/2023/12-billion-euro-fine-facebook-result-edpb-binding-decision_en

European Free Trade Association (EFTA). (n.d.-a). *The European Free Trade Association.* Retrieved June 25, 2025, from https://www.efta.int/about-efta/european-free-trade-association

European Free Trade Association (EFTA). (n.d.-b). *About EFTA.* Retrieved June 25, 2025, from https://www.efta.int/about-efta

European Free Trade Association (EFTA). (n.d.-c). *Legal documents.* Retrieved June 25, 2025, from https://www.efta.int/about-efta/legal-documents

European Union. (n.d.). *EU-Vietnam trade agreement. Standards and values.* Retrieved February 20, 2025, from https://circabc.europa.eu/ui/group/09242a36-a438–40fd-a7af-fe32e36cbd0e/library/d9bcaa49–3b0d-4da0–9294-f227159b8c16/details

Fairtrade International. (n.d.). *What is fairtrade?* Retrieved July 28, 2025, from https://www.fairtrade.net

Fast Retailing Co., Ltd. (2024). *FY2024 full-year financial results summary.* Retrieved May 2025 from https://www.fastretailing.com/eng/ir/news/2410101800.html#:~:text=%E2%96%A0FY2024%20consolidated%20results%3A%20Fast%20Retailing%20reports%20considerable%20full-year,yen%20and%20operating%20profit%20surpasses%20500%20billion%20yen

Federal Ministry of Labour and Social Affairs. (n.d.). *Act on corporate due diligence obligations in supply chains.* Retrieved February 20, 2025, from https://www.bmas.de/EN/Europe-and-the-World/International/Supply-Chain-Act/supply-chain-act.html

Finlay, R. (2010). *The pilgrim art: Cultures of porcelain in world history.* University of California Press.

Fletcher, R. A. (2006). *Moorish Spain*. University of California Press.

Forest Stewardship Council (FSC). (n.d.). *What's in a label?* Retrieved July 28, 2025, from https://fsc.org/en/label

Fortra. (2019, January 21). *Google fined $57M by data protection watchdog over GDPR violations*. https://www.digitalguardian.com/blog/google-fined-57m-data-protection-watchdog-over-gdpr-violations

French Ministry for Europe and Foreign Affairs. (2017). *New law on the duty of vigilance of parent companies and on its affiliated entities*. Retrieved February 20, 2025, from https://www.diplomatie.gouv.fr/IMG/pdf/law_on_the_duty_of_vigilance_cle8b1211.pdf

Friedman, T. L. (2005). *The world is flat: A brief history of the twenty-first century*. Farrar, Straus and Giroux.

Friedman, V. (2023, April 24). Rana Plaza collapse anniversary: What has changed in 10 years? *The New York Times*. https://www.nytimes.com/2023/04/24/fashion/rana-plaza-anniversary.html

GermanChambers of Commerce. (n.d.). *The German Chambers of Commerce Abroad (AHKs)*. Retrieved July 27, 2025, from https://www.ahk.de/en/

German Economic Team. (2024, April 12). *Restored shipping route in the Black Sea*. https://www.german-economic-team.com/en/newsletter/restored-shipping-route-in-the-black-sea/

Goldberg, P. K., & Reed, T. (2023). *Trade, disrupted. Finance & Development, 60*(2). International Monetary Fund. https://www.elibrary.imf.org/downloadpdf/journals/022/0060/002/022.0060.issue-002-en.pdf

Goodera. (2025, May 2). *12 Inspiring corporate social responsibility examples from brands in action*. Retrieved June 11, 2025, from https://www.goodera.com/blog/corporate-social-responsibility-examples

Government of Canada. (n.d.). *Comprehensive and progressive agreement for trans-Pacific partnership (CPTPP)*. Retrieved July 28, 2025, from https://www.international.gc.ca/trade-commerce/trade-agreements-accords-commerciaux/agr-acc/cptpp-ptpgp/index.aspx?lang=eng

Grant, R. M. (2021). *Contemporary strategy analysis* (11th ed.). Wiley.

The Guardian. (2011a, April 20). Japanese earthquake and tsunami causes fall in exports. *The Guardian*. https://www.theguardian.com/business/2011/apr/20/japanese-disasters-cause-fall-in-exports

The Guardian. (2011b, October 25). *Thailand's devastating floods are hitting PC hard drive supplies, warn analysts*. https://www.theguardian.com/technology/2011/oct/25/thailand-floods-hard-drive-shortage.

The Guardian. (2024, August 27). Canada to follow US lead in imposing 100% tariff on Chinese electric vehicles. *The Guardian*. Retrieved July 27, 2025, from https://www.theguardian.com/world/article/2024/aug/26/canada-tariff-china-electric-vehicles

Gürses, Ö. (2023). *Marine insurance law* (3rd ed.). Routledge.

Harvard Business School Online. (2019, June 6). *6 Examples of corporate social responsibility that were successful*. Retrieved June 11, 2025, from https://online.hbs.edu/blog/post/corporate-social-responsibility-examples

The Hague Centre for Strategic Studies. (2023). *Strategic raw materials for defence: Mapping European industry needs*. https://hcss.nl/wp-content/uploads/2023/01/Strategic-Raw-Materials-for-Defence-HCSS-2023-V2.pdf

Hill, C. W. L. (2023). *International business: Competing in the global marketplace* (14th ed.). McGraw-Hill Education.

Hitt, M. A., Ireland, R. D., & Hoskisson, R. E. (2023). *Strategic management: Concepts and cases – Competitiveness and globalization* (14th ed.). Cengage.

Holland, O. (2023, April 23). 10 Years after Rana Plaza, is Bangladesh's garment industry any safer? *CNN*. https://edition.cnn.com/style/article/rana-plaza-garment-worker-rights-accord/index.html

Houser, K. A., & Voss, W. G. (2018). GDPR: The end of Google and Facebook or a new paradigm in data privacy? *Richmond Journal of Law and Technology*,*25*(1).https://jolt.richmond.edu/gdpr-the-end-of-google-and-facebook-or-a-new-paradigm-in-data-privacy/

Hudson, G. N., & Madge, T. (2013). *The Institute clauses: A guide to the Institute cargo clauses* (3rd ed.). Informa Law.

Hunt, K. (2023, April 24). A decade after Rana Plaza collapse, garment workers are still fighting for their rights. *CNN*. https://edition.cnn.com/style/article/rana-plaza-garment-worker-rights-accord/index.html

International Chamber of Commerce (ICC). (2007). *UCP 600: Uniform customs and practice for documentary credits*. ICC Publication No. 600. ICC.

International Chamber of Commerce (ICC). (2010). *Sets of guidance papers on recommended principles and usages around UCP 600 rules*. https://iccwbo.org/wp-content/uploads/sites/3/2023/03/Set-of-Guidance-Papers-on-Recommended-Principles-and-Usages-around-UCP600-Rules.pdf

International Chamber of Commerce (ICC). (2019a). *Incoterms 2020 wall chart*. https://es.kuehne-nagel.com/documents/325959/325975/Knowledge-Incoterms-Graphic–2020.pdf/c9661fce-1c6e-f64a-e0d5–87f1272f800c?t=1618825992632

International Chamber of Commerce (ICC). (2019b). *Incoterms 2020*. ICC Publication.

International Chamber of Commerce (ICC). (2022). *Incoterms 2020 checklist and flowcharts*. https://icc.se/wp-content/uploads/2022/05/icc-incoterms-2020-checklist-int.pdf

International Chamber of Commerce (ICC). (2024, June 24). *ICC dispute resolution statistics 2023*. Retrieved July 28, 2025, from https://iccwbo.org/news-publications/news/icc-dispute-resolution-statistics-2023/

International Chamber of Commerce (ICC). (n.d.-a). *About ICC*. https://iccwbo.org/about-us/

International Chamber of Commerce (ICC). (n.d.-b). *Incoterms 2020*. https://iccwbo.org/business-solutions/incoterms-rules/incoterms-2020/

International Chamber of Commerce (ICC). (n.d.-c). *Arbitration clause*. https://iccwbo.org/dispute-resolution/dispute-resolution-services/arbitration/rules-procedure/arbitration-clause/

International Federation of Organic Agriculture Movements (IFOAM). (2020). *The world of organic agriculture: Statistics and emerging trends 2020*. IFOAM–Organics International. https://orgprints.org/id/eprint/37222/9/willer-et-al-2020-full-document-2020-02-28-4th-corrigenda.pdf

International Federation of Organic Agriculture Movements (IFOAM). (n.d.). *About us*. Retrieved July 28, 2025, from https://www.ifoam.bio/about-us

International Institute for Management Development (IMD). (2025, June). *IMD world competitiveness ranking 2025*. IMD World Competitiveness Center. Retrieved July 27, 2025, from https://www.imd.org/centers/wcc/world-competitiveness-center/rankings/world-competitiveness-ranking/

International Institute for the Unification of Private Law (UNIDROIT). (2016). *UNIDROIT principles of international commercial contracts 2016*. https://www.unidroit.org/english/principles/contracts/principles2016/principles2016-e.pdf

International Labour Organization. (n.d.). *The Rana Plaza disaster ten years on: What has changed?*. ILO. Retrieved June 11, 2025, from https://webapps.ilo.org/infostories/en-GB/Stories/Country-Focus/rana-plaza

International Monetary Fund. (n.d.). *About the IMF.* https://www.imf.org/en/About

International Organization for Standardization (ISO). (n.d.). *ISO 14000 family – Environmental management.* Retrieved July 28, 2025, from https://www.iso.org/standards/popular/iso-14000-family

International Trade Administration, US Department of Commerce. (n.d.). *Prohibited and restricted imports: South Africa – Country commercial guide.* Retrieved July 21, 2025, from https://www.trade.gov/country-commercial-guides/south-africa-prohibited-and-restricted-imports

International Trade Centre. (n.d.). *Who we are.* https://www.intracen.org/about-us/who-we-are

International Trade Council. (2023). *The evolution of international trade.* https://tradecouncil.org/wp-content/uploads/2024/10/The-Evolution-of-International-Trade.pdf

Japan Customs. (n.d.-a). *Articles prohibited from importation/exportation.* Retrieved July 21, 2025, from https://www.customs.go.jp/english/c-answer_e/customs answer_e.htm#kinsei

Japan Customs. (n.d.-b). *Procedure for import/export declaration.* Retrieved July 21, 2025, from https://www.customs.go.jp/english/procedures/index_pf.htm

Japan External Trade Organization. (n.d.). *What is JETRO.* https://www.jetro.go.jp/en/

Johnson, G., Scholes, K., & Whittington, R. (2020). *Exploring strategy: Text and cases* (12th ed.). Pearson.

Kotler, P., & Keller, K. L. (2016). *Marketing management* (15th ed.). Pearson Education.

Krugman, P. (2022). *International economics: Theory and policy* (11th ed.). Pearson.

Krugman, P. R. (1979). Increasing returns, monopolistic competition, and international trade. *Journal of International Economics*, *9*(4), 469–479.

Krugman, P. R. (1980). Scale economies, product differentiation, and the pattern of trade. *American Economic Review*, *70*(5), 950–959.

Krugman, P. R., Obstfeld, M., & Melitz, M. J. (2022). *International economics: Theory and policy* (12th ed.). Pearson.

Kuehne+Nagel. (n.d.). *Incoterms 2020 – your guide to international trade regulations.* https://es.kuehne-nagel.com/es/-/informacion/incoterms

Landler, M., & Barboza, D. (2006, August 2). Wal-Mart finds that its formula doesn't fit every culture. *The New York Times.* https://www.nytimes.com/2006/08/02/business/worldbusiness/02walmart.html

Lasserre, P., & Monteiro, F. (2022). *Global strategic management* (5th ed.). Bloomsbury Publishing.

Lee, K. Y. (2000). *From third world to first: The Singapore story: 1965–2000.* HarperCollins.

London Court of International Arbitration (LCIA). (n.d.). *Recommended clauses.* https://lcia.org/Dispute_Resolution_Services/LCIA_Recommended_Clauses.aspx lcia.org

London Market Association. (n.d.). *Cargo clauses project.* Retrieved July 21, 2025, from https://www.lmalloyds.com/lma/underwriting/marine/JCC/JCC_Clauses_Project/Cargo_Clauses.aspx

LVMH. (2023). *Annual report 2022.* https://lvmh-com.cdn.prismic.io/lvmh-com/ZmcHwJm069VX1mke_lvmh_document-financier-2022_uk-final.pdf

Mankiw, N. G. (2021). *Principles of economics* (9th ed.). Cengage Learning.

Marine Stewardship Council (MSC). (n.d.). *Our approach.* Retrieved July 28, 2025, from https://www.msc.org/what-we-are-doing/our-approach

McDonald's. (2023). *2022 Annual report.* https://corporate.mcdonalds.com/content/dam/sites/corp/nfl/pdf/MCD_2023_Annual_Report.pdf

MERCOSUR. (n.d.). *What is MERCOSUR?* Retrieved June 25, 2025, from https://www.mercosur.int/en/about-mercosur/mercosur-in-brief/

Miller, C., & Venugopalan, V. (2025, June). *Apple supply chain report.* American Enterprise Institute. https://www.aei.org/wp-content/uploads/2025/06/RPT_Miller_Apple-Supply-Chain_June-2025.pdf

Ministry of Commerce of the People's Republic of China. (n.d.). *About MOFCOM.* http://english.mofcom.gov.cn/

Ministry of Economy, Trade and Industry, Japan. (n.d.). *About METI.* https://www.meti.go.jp/english/

Ministry of Trade and Industry, Singapore (MTI). (n.d.-a). *About MTI.* https://www.mti.gov.sg/About-Us/About-MTI

Ministry of Trade and Industry, Singapore (MTI). (n.d.-b). *Comprehensive and progressive agreement for trans-Pacific partnership (CPTPP)-.* Government of Singapore. Retrieved July 28, 2025, from https://www.mti.gov.sg/Trade/Free-Trade-Agreements/CPTPP

Ministry of Trade and Industry, Singapore (MTI). (n.d.-c). *Free trade agreements.* Retrieved July 28, 2025, from https://www.mti.gov.sg/Trade/Free-Trade-Agreements

Moses, M. L. (2017). *The principles and practice of international commercial arbitration* (3rd ed.). Cambridge University Press.

MSIG Insurance (Hong Kong) Limited. (n.d.). *Cover comparison between Institute Cargo Clauses (A), (B), and (C).* Retrieved July 21, 2025, from https://www.msig.com.hk/sites/msig_hk/files/Cover%20comparison%20between%20ICC%20%28A%29%28B%29%28C%29%20_1.pdf

Murray, C., Holloway, D., & Timson-Hunt, D. (2018). *Schmitthoff's export trade: The law and practice of international trade* (12th ed.). Sweet & Maxwell.

National Bureau of Economic Research (NBER). (2024). *Supply chain disruptions and pandemic-era inflation.* https://www.nber.org/digest/202404/supply-chain-disruptions-and-pandemic-era-inflation

National Geographic Education. (n.d.). *Tohoku earthquake and tsunami.* National Geographic Society. https://education.nationalgeographic.org/resource/tohoku-earthquake-and-tsunami/

National Geographic Society. (2024, February 10). *The silk road.* https://education.nationalgeographic.org/resource/silk-road/

New Zealand Ministry of Foreign Affairs and Trade (MFAT). (n.d.). *Comprehensive and progressive agreement for trans-Pacific partnership (CPTPP).* Retrieved July 28, 2025, from https://www.mfat.govt.nz/en/trade/free-trade-agreements/free-trade-agreements-in-force/cptpp

NHK World-Japan. (2025, March 10). *Lessons from Tohoku: 14 years since the giant earthquake.* https://www3.nhk.or.jp/nhkworld/en/news/backstories/3869/

Nike. (2023). *Fiscal 2023 fourth quarter and full year results.* https://investors.nike.com/investors/news-events-and-reports/investor-news/investor-news-details/2023/NIKE-Inc.-Reports-Fiscal-2023-Fourth-Quarter-and-Full-Year-Results/default.aspx

Nikkei Asia. (2020, October 15). *Japan expands 'China exit' subsidies for moves to Southeast.* https://asia.nikkei.com/Politics/Japan-expands-China-exit-subsidies-for-moves-to-Southeast-Asia

Nikkei Asia. (2021, September 15). *Toyota ditches signature 'just-in-time' to fight chip.* https://asia.nikkei.com/Business/Automobiles/Toyota-ditches-signature-just-in-time-to-fight-chip-crunch

Norman, L., & Pancevski, B. (2025, July 18). EU targets Russia with toughest sanctions package in years. *The Wall Street Journal.* https://www.wsj.com/world/europe/eu-targets-russia-with-toughest-sanctions-package-in-years-59e49926

Observatory of Economic Complexity (OEC). (n.d.-a). *Corn*. Retrieved July 27, 2025, from https://oec.world/en/profile/hs/corn

Observatory of Economic Complexity (OEC). (n.d.-b). *Cotton*. Retrieved July 27, 2025, from https://oec.world/en/profile/hs/cotton

Observatory of Economic Complexity (OEC). (n.d.-c). *Poultry meat*. Retrieved July 27, 2025, from https://oec.world/en/profile/hs/poultry-meat

Observatory of Economic Complexity (OEC). (n.d.-d). *Raw sugar*. Retrieved July 27, 2025, from https://oec.world/en/profile/hs/raw-sugar

Observatory of Economic Complexity (OEC). (n.d.-e). *Rice*. Retrieved July 27, 2025, from https://oec.world/en/profile/hs/rice

Observatory of Economic Complexity (OEC). (n.d.-f). *Russia*. Retrieved July 27, 2025, from https://oec.world/en/profile/country/rus

Observatory of Economic Complexity (OEC). (n.d.-g). *Soybeans*. Retrieved July 27, 2025, from https://oec.world/en/profile/hs/soybeans

Observatory of Economic Complexity (OEC). (n.d.-h). *Spices*. Retrieved July 27, 2025, from https://oec.world/en/profile/hs/spices

Observatory of Economic Complexity (OEC). (n.d.-i). *Ukraine*. Retrieved July 27, 2025, from https://oec.world/en/profile/country/ukr

Observatory of Economic Complexity (OEC). (n.d.-j). *Wheat*. Retrieved July 27, 2025, from https://oec.world/en/profile/hs/wheat

OECD. (2021). *Effective carbon rates 2021: Pricing carbon emissions through taxes and emissions trading*. OECD Publishing. https://www.oecd.org/content/dam/oecd/en/publications/reports/2021/05/effective-carbon-rates-2021_02959cc3/0e8e24f5-en.pdf

OECD. (2023). *International trade in the wake of multiple shocks*. OECD Publishing. https://www.oecd.org/content/dam/oecd/en/publications/reports/2023/11/international-trade-in-the-wake-of-multiple-shocks_b3774c15/9288b5bf-en.pdf

Office of the United States Trade Representative. (n.d.-a). *About us*. https://ustr.gov/about-us

Office of the United States Trade Representative (n.d.-b). *Economic community of West African states (ECOWAS)*. https://ustr.gov/countries-regions/africa/regional-economic-communities-rec/economic-community-west-african-states

Office of the United States Trade Representative. (n.d.-c). *United States-Mexico-Canada agreement*. https://ustr.gov/trade-agreements/free-trade-agreements/united-states-mexico-canada-agreement

Our World in Data. (n.d.). *Trade as a share of GDP*. Retrieved July 21, 2025, from https://ourworldindata.org/grapher/trade-as-share-of-gdp?tab=chart&country=OWID_WRL~CHN~USA~SGP

Paton, E. (2023, April 24). A Grim anniversary for survivors of the Rana Plaza disaster. *The New York Times*. https://www.nytimes.com/2023/04/24/fashion/rana-plaza-anniversary.html

Peng, M. W., & Meyer, K. E. (2023). *Global strategy* (5th ed.). Cengage.

Piltz, B. (2020a). *Differences between Incoterms® 2010 and 2020 (Webinar)*. Khuehne+Nagel. https://register.gotowebinar.com/recording/8653024974975372045

Piltz, B. (2020b). *Incoterms® 2020 in Detail (Webinar)*. Khuehne+Nagel. https://register.gotowebinar.com/recording/3022171941970978828

Piltz, B. (2021). *Understanding Incoterms 2020® (Webinar)*. Khuehne+Nagel. https://register.gotowebinar.com/recording/2698744446301294l0

Pinsent Masons. (2024, June 11). LCIA statistics show doubling arbitration parties from Africa. *Out-Law News*. Retrieved July 28, 2025, from https://www.pinsentmasons.com/out-law/news/lcia-statistics-show-doubling-arbitration-parties-africa Pinsent Masonsfaegredrinker.com

Polanyi, K. (1944). *The great transformation: The political and economic origins of our time*. Beacon Press.

Pons, C., & Reid, H. (2024, November 20). Inditex boosts fast-fashion flights from India to avoid shipping delays. *Reuters*. https://www.reuters.com/business/retail-consumer/inditex-boosts-fast-fashion-flights-india-avoid-shipping-delays-2024-11-20

Porter, M. E. (1985). *Competitive advantage: Creating and sustaining superior performance*. Free Press.

Porter, M. E. (1990). *The competitive advantage of nations*. Free Press.

Porter, M. E. (1996). What is strategy? *Harvard Business Review*, *74*(6), 61–78.

PricewaterhouseCoopers (PwC). (n.d.). *ESG reporting and preparation of a sustainability report*. Retrieved July 28, 2025, from https://www.pwc.com/sk/en/environmental-social-and-corporate-governance-esg/esg-reporting.html

Qatar Airways. (n.d.). *Enjoy the most memorable flying experience in the worlds*. https://www.qatarairways.com/en-th/onboard/qsuite.html?iid=ALL29648260

Rainforest Alliance. (n.d.). *Our mission and work*. Retrieved July 28, 2025, from https://www.rainforest-alliance.org

RetailDetail. (2024, April 11). Uniqlo beats the current, raises profit forecast. *RetailDetail*. https://www.retaildetail.eu/news/fashion/uniqlo-beats-the-current-raises-profit-forecast/

Reuters. (2023, May 31). *Turkish lira 1-yr implied volatility gauge hits highest in at least 15 years*. https://www.reuters.com/markets/currencies/turkish-lira-1-yr-implied-volatility-gauge-hits-highest-least-15-years-2023-05-31/

Reuters. (2024a, February 1). *Tesla to bring LFP battery supply chain to US*. https://www.reuters.com/business/autos-transportation/tesla-bring-lfp-battery-supply-chain-us-bloomberg-news-reporter-2024-01-31/

Reuters. (2024b, July 4). China's BYD opens EV factory in Thailand, first in Southeast Asia. *Channel News Asia*. https://www.reuters.com/business/autos-transportation/chinas-byd-opens-ev-factory-thailand-first-southeast-asia-2024-07-04/

Reuters. (2025a, April 11). EU, China will look into setting minimum prices on electric vehicles. *Reuters*. Retrieved July 27, 2025, from https://www.reuters.com/business/autos-transportation/eu-china-start-talks-lifting-eu-tariffs-chinese-electric-vehicles-handelsblatt-2025-04-10/

Reuters. (2025b, April 7). *Trump strategy threatens critical mineral supplies for clean power*. https://www.reuters.com/business/energy/trump-strategy-threatens-critical-mineral-supplies-clean-power-2025-04-07/

Ricardo, D. (1817). *On the principles of political economy and taxation*. John Murray. https://socialsciences.mcmaster.ca/econ/ugcm/3ll3/ricardo/Principles.pdf

Rodrik, D. (2011). *The globalization paradox: Democracy and the future of the world economy*. W. W. Norton & Company.

Ryanair. (2024). *FY24 financial results presentation*. https://investor.ryanair.com/wp-content/uploads/2024/05/FY24-Ryanair-Results.pdf

Sachdev, V., & Rao, A. (2025, March 11). What happened the last time Trump imposed tariffs on steel and aluminum. *Reuters*. https://www.reuters.com/graphics/TRUMP-TARIFFS/STEEL/gdpznwgdzpw/

Samsung Electronics. (2023). *Annual report 2022*. https://img.global.news.samsung.com/es/wp-content/uploads/2023/09/Samsung-Annual-Report-2022_ENG.pdf

Samuelson, P. A., & Nordhaus, W. D. (2019). *Economics* (20th ed.). McGraw-Hill Education.

Schaffer, R., Agusti, F., Dhooge, L., & Berger-Walliser, G. (2025). *International business law and its environment* (11th ed.). Cengage.

Sen, A. (1999). *Development as freedom*. Alfred A. Knopf.

Sen, A., Fitoussi, J. P., & Stiglitz, J. E. (2010). *Mismeasuring our lives: Why GDP doesn't add up*. The New Press.

Seyoum, B. (2021). *Export–import theory, practices, and procedures* (4th ed.). Routledge.

Singapore Airlines. (n.d.). *Enjoy the ultimate Business Class experience*. https://www.singaporeair.com/en-sg/business-class-flights-singapore-airlines?msockid=3a1398039907628d3aad8df098676312

Singapore Business Federation. (n.d.). *About us*. https://sbf.org.sg/about-us

Singapore Customs. (n.d.). *Controlled & prohibited goods for import*. Retrieved July 21, 2025, from https://www.customs.gov.sg/businesses/importing-goods/controlled-and-prohibited-goods-for-import/

Singapore International Arbitration Centre (SIAC). (2026). *SIAC model clause*. https://siac.org.sg/siac-model-clause

Singapore International Commercial Court. (n.d.). *About the SICC*. https://www.sicc.gov.sg/

Skytrax. (2024). *World airline awards 2024: 5-Star airlines*. https://skytraxratings.com/the-worlds-5-star-airlines

Smith, A. (1776). *An inquiry into the nature and causes of the wealth of nations*. https://socialsciences.mcmaster.ca/econ/ugcm/3ll3/smith/wealth/index.html

SMP Global. (n.d.). *Incoterms 2020*. https://smp-global.com/incoterms/

Social Accountability International (SAI). (n.d.). *SA8000® standard*. Retrieved July 28, 2025, from https://sa-intl.org/programs/sa8000/

Starbucks. (n.d.). *C.A.F.E. practices ethical sourcing program*. Retrieved July 28, 2025, from https://www.starbucks.com/responsibility/sourcing/coffee

Statista. (2023). *Leading freight transportation companies worldwide in 2022, based on freight revenue*. https://www.statista.com/statistics/503884/leading-freight-transportation-firms-worldwide/

Statista. (2024). *Net profit of Ryanair from 2010 to 2024 (in million euros)*. https://www.statista.com/statistics/756093/ryanair-net-profit/

Stehrer, R. (2025, March 19). *What is behind the US trade deficit?* The Vienna Institute for International Economic Studies. https://wiiw.ac.at/what-is-behind-the-us-trade-deficit-n-673.html

Stiglitz, J. E. (2002). *Globalization and its discontents*. W. W. Norton & Company.

Stiglitz, J. E. (2007). *Making globalization work*. W. W. Norton & Company.

Stiglitz, J. E., Sen, A., & Fitoussi, J. P. (2009). *The measurement of economic performance and social progress*. Retrieved July 21, 2025, from https://ec.europa.eu/eurostat/documents/8131721/8131772/Stiglitz-Sen-Fitoussi-Commission-report.pdf

Swiss Arbitration Association (SAC). (2024, April 3). *Update from the Swiss Arbitration Centre*. Retrieved July 28, 2025, from https://www.swissarbitration.org/update-from-the-swiss-arbitration-centre-3/HFW+3Wikipedia+3Lexology+3

Teh, R., Keck, A., Nee, C., & Escaith, H. (2011, April 28). Japan's earthquake and tsunami: International trade and global supply chain impacts. *VoxEU.org*. https://cepr.org/voxeu/columns/japans-earthquake-and-tsunami-international-trade-and-global-supply-chain-impacts

Thai Customs Department. (n.d.). *Tariff nomenclature and HS classification database*. http://itd.customs.go.th/igtf/th/main_frame.jsp?lang=th&top_menu=menu_homepage&current_id=5028

Thailand Board of Investment. (2023). *Opportunities and support measures for EV activities*. https://www.boi.go.th/upload/content/20230706%20EN%20BOI_.pdf

Thompson, A. A., Peteraf, M. A., Gamble, J. E., & Strickland, A. J. III. (2024). *Crafting and executing strategy: The quest for competitive advantage* (24th ed.). McGraw-Hill Education.

Thompson, B. (2025). *Incoterms® 2020 explained – The complete guide*. https://incodocs.com/blog/incoterms-2020-explained-the-complete-guide/

Toyota Motor Corporation. (2023). *Financial summary FY2023*. https://global.toyota/pages/global_toyota/ir/financial-results/2023_4q_summary_en.pdf

Trade Finance Global. (2025). *A complete guide to Incoterms® 2020 rules (international commerce terms)*. https://www.tradefinanceglobal.com/incoterms/

Triolo, P. (n.d.). The evolution of China's semiconductor industry under U.S. export controls. *American Affairs Journal*. Retrieved July 23, 2025, from https://americanaffairsjournal.org/2024/11/the-evolution-of-chinas-semiconductor-industry-under-u-s-export-controls/

Udomkit, N., Ensslin, V., & Meinhold, R. (2020). Three stages of trust building of international small- and medium-sized enterprises. *Global Business Review*, *21*(4), 906–917. https://doi.org/10.1177/0972150919857015

UK Judiciary. (n.d.). *The commercial court*. https://www.judiciary.uk/courts-and-tribunals/business-and-property-courts/commercial-court/#:~:text=The%20Commercial%20Court%20specialises%20in%20the%20determination%20of,to%20the%20Civil%20Procedure%20Rules%20and%20other%20guidance

UNCITRAL. (2016). *Guide on the convention on the recognition and enforcement of foreign arbitral awards (New York, 1958)*. https://uncitral.un.org/sites/uncitral.un.org/files/media-documents/uncitral/en/2016_guide_on_the_convention.pdf

Ungphakorn, P. (n.d.). *The quality of life of a southeast Asian: A chronicle of hope (from womb to tomb)*. Retrieved July 28, 2025, from https://www.nectec.or.th/users/htk/dr-puey/womb-tomb.html

United Nations. (2010). *United Nations convention on contracts for the international sale of goods*. https://uncitral.un.org/sites/uncitral.un.org/files/media-documents/uncitral/en/19-09951_e_ebook.pdf

United Nations. (2023, October 10). Commodity-dependent states underperforming in development, expert warns at joint meeting of Second Committee, Economic and Social Council (Press Release GA/EF/3589-ECOSOC/7146). *United Nations*. Retrieved July 20, 2025, from https://press.un.org/en/2023/gaef3589.doc.htm

United Nations Conference on Trade and Development (UNCTAD). (2024a, February 22). Navigating troubled waters: Impact on global trade from disruption of shipping routes in the Red Sea and Black Sea. *United Nations Conference on Trade and Development*. https://unctad.org/publication/navigating-troubled-waters-impact-global-trade-disruption-shipping-routes-red-sea-black

United Nations Conference on Trade and Development (UNCTAD). (2024b, December 19). *Enhancing supply chain resilience amid rising global risks*. https://unctad.org/news/enhancing-supply-chain-resilience-amid-rising-global-risks

United Nations Conference on Trade and Development (UNCTAD). (2024c). Key statistics and trends in international trade 2023. *United Nations Conference on Trade and Development*. Retrieved July 21, 2025, from https://unctad.org/system/files/official-document/ditctab2024d1_en.pdf

United Nations Conference on Trade and Development. (n.d.). *About UN trade and development (UNCTAD)*. https://unctad.org/about

United States International Trade Commission. (2024). *Harmonized tariff schedule of the United States (2025)*. https://hts.usitc.gov

US Chamber of Commerce. (n.d.). *About the U.S. Chamber*. https://www.uschamber.com/about-us

US Customs and Border Protection. (2023). *Uyghur Forced Labor Prevention Act (UFLPA)*. https://www.cbp.gov/trade/forced-labor/UFLPA

US Department of Commerce. (2024, December 2). *Commerce strengthens export controls to restrict China's capability to produce advanced semiconductors for military use*. US Department of Commerce. Retrieved July 23, 2025, from https://www.bis.gov/press-release/commerce-strengthens-export-controls-restrict-chinas-capability-produce-advanced-semiconductors-military

US Department of Commerce. (n.d.). *International trade administration*. https://www.trade.gov/about-us

US Environmental Protection Agency. (n.d.). *Energy star*. Retrieved July 28, 2025, from https://www.energystar.gov

Van de Graaf, T. (2023). *The geopolitics of energy after Russia's war in Ukraine*. Fondation Jean-Jaurès. https://www.jean-jaures.org/wp-content/uploads/2023/10/Forging_Europes_Leadership.pdf

Verbeke, A., & Lee, I. (2022). *International business strategy: Rethinking the foundations of global corporate success* (2nd ed.). Cambridge University Press.

Wheelen, L., & Hunger, D. Bentley, A., & Bamford, C. (2020). *Strategic management and business policy: Globalization, innovation, and sustainability* (15th ed.). Pearson.

Wolf, M. (2004). *Why globalization works*. Yale University Press.

World Bank Group. (2020). *The African continental free trade area: Economic and distributional effects*. https://www.worldbank.org/en/topic/trade/publication/the-african-continental-free-trade-area

World Bank Group. (2023). *State and trends of carbon pricing 2023*. World Bank. https://documents1.worldbank.org/curated/en/099805106052321586/pdf/IDU0df4b14850029d0403c0811b0f1575605c07a.pdf

World Bank Group. (n.d.-a). *GDP (current US$)*. Retrieved July 21, 2025, from https://data.worldbank.org/indicator/NY.GDP.MKTP.CD?end=2024&start=2024&view=map

World Bank Group. (n.d.-b). *Singapore overview*. https://www.worldbank.org/en/country/singapore/overview

World Bank Group. (n.d.-c). *Who we are*. https://www.worldbank.org/ext/en/who-we-are

World Bank Group. (n.d.-d). *World development indicators: Exports and imports of goods and services (current US$)*. The World Bank Group. https://data.worldbank.org/indicator/NE.EXP.GNFS.CD

World Bank Group. (n.d.-e). *World development indicators: Trade (% of GDP)*. https://data.worldbank.org/indicator/NE.TRD.GNFS.ZS

World Bank Group. (n.d.-f). *Doing business*. World Bank. Retrieved July 28, 2025, from https://archive.doingbusiness.org/en/data/exploretopics/trading-across-borders

World Customs Organization (WCO). (2023, March). *Effective enforcement of international trade regulations requires powerful data analytics*. https://mag.wcoomd.org/magazine/wco-news-1000-issue-1–2023/effective-enforcement-of-international-trade-regulations-requires-powerful-data-analytics/

World Customs Organization (WCO). (n.d.-a). *Discover the WCO*. https://www.wcoomd.org/en/about-us/what-is-the-wco/discover-the-wco.aspx

World Customs Organization (WCO). (n.d.-b). *Harmonized system nomenclature 2022 edition*. https://www.wcoomd.org/en/topics/nomenclature/instrument-and-tools/hs-nomenclature-2022-edition/hs-nomenclature-2022-edition.aspx

World Customs Organization (WCO). (n.d.-c). *What is the harmonized system (HS)?* https://www.wcoomd.org/en/topics/nomenclature/overview/what-is-the-harmonized-system.aspx

World Economic Forum (WEF). (2020, December 16). Global competitiveness report special edition 2020: How countries are performing on the road to recovery. *World Economic Forum*. Retrieved July 27, 2025, from https://www.weforum.org/publications/the-global-competitiveness-report-2020/

World Economic Forum (WEF). (2021, May 18). *An expert explains: What is RCEP, the world's biggest trade deal?* https://www.weforum.org/stories/2021/05/rcep-world-biggest-trade-deal/
World Economic Forum (WEF). (2023, January). *AfCFTA: A new era for global business and investment in Africa.* https://www.weforum.org/whitepapers/afcfta-a-new-era-for-global-business-and-investment-in-africa/
World Economic Forum (WEF). (n.d.). *Future-proofing global value chains: Country preparedness and beyond.* https://www.weforum.org/projects/reshaping-global-value/
Worldometer. (n.d.). *GDP by country.* Retrieved July 21, 2025, from https://www.worldometers.info/gdp/gdp-by-country/
World Trade Organization (WTO). (2023a). *Global value chain development report 2023: Resilient and sustainable GVCs in turbulent times.* https://www.wto.org/english/res_e/booksp_e/gvc_dev_rep23_e.pdf
World Trade Organization (WTO). (2023b). *World trade statistical review 2023.* WTO Publications. https://www.wto.org/english/res_e/publications_e/wtsr_2023_e.htm
World Trade Organization (WTO). (2025). *Global trade outlook and statistics.* WTO. https://www.wto.org/english/news_e/news25_e/stat_07oct25_e.pdf
World Trade Organization (WTO). (n.d.-a). *The WTO: Overview.* https://www.wto.org/english/thewto_e/whatis_e/wto_dg_stat_e.htm
World Trade Organization (WTO). (n.d.-b). *Understanding the WTO.* https://www.wto.org/english/thewto_e/whatis_e/tif_e/tif_e.htm
World Trade Organization (WTO). (n.d.-c). *History of the multilateral trading system.* WTO. https://www.wto.org/english/thewto_e/history_e/history_e.htm

INDEX

Note: Page numbers in *italics* indicate figures, page numbers in **bold** indicate tables in the text, and references following "n" refer to the notes.

Verlag GmbH, Kaufingerstraße 24, 80331 München, Germany

For Product Safety Concerns and Information please contact our EU representative GPSR@taylorandfrancis.com Taylor & Francis Verlag GmbH, Kaufingerstraße 24, 80331 München, Germany